Up The Creek Without a Paddle

TAMMY COHEN

Up The Creek Without a Paddle

**THE TRUE STORY OF JOHN AND ANNE DARWIN:
THE MAN WHO 'DIED' AND THE WIFE WHO LIED**

JOHN BLAKE

Published by John Blake Publishing Ltd,
3 Bramber Court, 2 Bramber Road,
London W14 9PB, England

www.johnblakepublishing.co.uk

First published in hardback in 2008

ISBN: 978 1 84454 632 9

British Library Cataloguing-in-Publication Data:

A catalogue record for this book is available from the British Library.

Design by www.envydesign.co.uk

Printed in the UK by CPI William Clowes Beccles NR34 7TL

1 3 5 7 9 10 8 6 4 2

Papers used by John Blake Publishing are natural, recyclable products made
from wood grown in sustainable forests. The manufacturing processes conform to
the environmental regulations of the country of origin.

CONTENTS

PROLOGUE
21 MARCH 2002

If you were to send a picture postcard of your hols to anyone, it probably wouldn't be of Seaton Carew in the off-peak season. The wide sandy beach, so bustling in summertime, seems to stretch on endlessly into the gloom of an overcast winter's day, sand merging with sky in a never-ending wash of grey. Running along the beach is the promenade linking Seaton Carew with Hartlepool's trendy new marina to the north, but with the sun in short supply few people brave the notorious North Sea winds to enjoy the scenic coastal walk. Apparently, if you're lucky you can see seals bathing just off the shoreline to the south on Seal Sands but on a gloomy day in mid March no one wants to linger, straining their eyes across the murky sea.

Once an upmarket resort with a hugely popular funfair, plus a whole host of fish and chip shops, where queues of day-trippers used to snake straight out of the doors in the high season, Seaton Carew has largely fallen into a state of neglect. Its once brightly painted façades now give off an apologetic, grubby-round-the-edges look, like children's faces ingrained with dirt.

The golf course, which draws players from all around on fine weekends when the rolling lawns give on to a sparkling sea, is all but deserted out of season, its flags fluttering forlornly in the chill breeze. Behind the seafront life goes quietly on around the modern estate built on land previously used to store props from local pits. Being 2002, the residents are as yet blissfully ignorant of the fact that their gardens are contaminated by arsenic, lead and zinc, or of the three-year battle that lies ahead to get someone to accept responsibility for cleaning them up. To the south, the hulking structure of Hartlepool nuclear power station bears brooding witness to the changing tides, protected by metre upon metre of barbed-wire fencing.

Cannes it ain't.

The Cliff in Seaton Carew boasts a terrace of large, stuccoed villas fronting the sea. In past centuries these would have been grand family residences or smart guesthouses for the well-heeled ladies and gentlemen of the north-east. Now the off-white paint is peeling and behind the once-elegant façades several buildings have been crudely divided up into studios and flats by thin plasterboard, destroying the high-ceilinged symmetry of the architecture. Their windows gaze out across the deep-black North Sea in dull resignation. An ever-changing tide of transient tenants drift in and out of residence, carrying their belongings with them in cardboard boxes.

Prologue

Ocean View (No. 2) is a guesthouse, its four bedrooms much in demand during the summer months by holidaymakers happy to wake every morning to the angry squawking of overhead seagulls. Mid-week in March it gives off an introspective air of self-protection, however.

No. 3 is a large, single-family home. With seven bedrooms, plus a draughty cellar and attic, it almost cries out for the sound of children shrieking or teenagers' doors slamming, the everyday noises of family life wafting up and down the sweeping stairwell, filling the spaces in the wide hallways. And yet just one middle-aged couple go about their business here, insular and unobtrusive, leaving hardly an imprint on the echoing emptiness of the house. Even their two dogs are measured and well-mannered, as if subdued by the orderliness of their surroundings.

Next door at No. 4 it's a different story altogether. Here the house has been divided up into bedsits where tenants lead their own separate lives behind firmly closed doors, scuttling through the communal areas, their heads already bent in search of keys.

Usually mid-week mornings are quiet here, with the residents either at work or holed up inside their homes, curtains half-drawn against the day, but on Thursday, 21 March 2002 there's movement at No. 3. The wide front door opens and a man emerges, blinking slightly in the dull daylight. He is dressed warmly, in a dark jacket, jeans and a hat, as befits the time of year, and he pauses briefly on the stone porch step while he gazes out to sea with narrowed, deep-set eyes.

Moments later he has passed through the small car park in

front of the house, where his black Range Rover stands idle. The man is proud of his car, with its personalised number plate, including the initials from his name JRD, and worries about the damage the sea air, threaded with salt and sand, could do to it. But this morning he walks on without a second glance.

And now he has crossed the wide road in front of the house and is making his way across the yawning sandy beach, but his progress is slow because he is carrying something under one arm – something so large and unwieldy it makes his body lean to the side as he struggles to counterbalance it. From a distance it could be mistaken for a surfboard, but on closer inspection it is revealed to be a kayak, made of lightweight fibreglass but still awkward to handle, particularly with the two sets of paddles he is also carrying. The kayak is red, its vivid colour blazing a blood-like trail across the dull yellow sand, made greyish by the blunt graininess of the light.

To anyone unused to sea sports, the idea of voluntarily taking to the freezing waters on a cool, early spring day might seem unimaginable to even the most determined surfer in the latest hi-tech wetsuit, yet around these parts no one would turn a hair. The locals are used to a steady procession of wind surfers, kite surfers, even the odd scuba diver, finding in these inhospitable waters a personal challenge they refuse to turn down. On several occasions the man has been seen, lugging his red kayak to the shoreline, seemingly oblivious to the wind blowing off the sea.

Truth be told, should paddling be your thing, today is a pretty good day for it. The sea, so terrifying when angry, sending monstrous waves that crash down on shrinking sands, is unusually calm. When you look out across the water, as the kayaker does for one moment when he reaches the surf, the surface appears flat and unbroken, gently undulating in the morning breeze. Inasmuch as conditions in this part of the world, at this time of year, can ever be considered perfect, now they appear so; no wonder the lone kayaker doesn't linger at the water's edge for long.

With a sudden sense of purpose, he thrusts his boat into the water and follows after it, swinging himself inside as soon as the underside is clear of the gently sloping sand. And then he is off, a solitary, slightly hunched figure flailing his paddle against the vast expanse of the ocean. Pretty soon his outline can no longer be detected from the shore, just the crimson slash of his kayak weaving through the murky water, like red stitching across a colourless cloth.

But then he disappears entirely from view behind the rocks to the south, the last ripples from his paddle swallowed up by the implacable tide. Now anyone who happens to be walking along the beach will simply see a clear, unsullied sheet of unusually still water.

It is as if he was never there.

1
MR AND MRS AVERAGE

'They're perfect.'

Anne Darwin shot a nervous look towards her husband, standing still on the beach beside her, his slightly hunched back turned towards to the sea as he gazed across the promenade and the road behind it at the row of cream-coloured villas directly facing them.

'They're absolutely perfect,' he repeated with a worrying air of finality.

Anne followed his gaze to the two adjoining four-storey, mid-terrace houses with their wide front porches, long, wrought-iron balconies and cavernous bay windows. Despite her misgivings, his obvious excitement was infectious. The houses were impressive, no doubt about it. And they'd long been entranced by the area, regularly making the 20-mile trip from their home in the village of Witton Gilbert, near Durham, to walk their dogs, Zena and Meg, on the wide sandy beach.

'Imagine waking up every morning to this view,' they'd muse, playing the 'what if?' game, as couples taking a stroll together somewhere in striking scenery often do.

'I'd be able to take the kayak out whenever I wanted,' John would say wistfully. 'And the dogs would love having all this on their doorstep.'

Of course there was the little matter of finance. At this stage, in 2000, the Darwins already owned about a dozen rental properties around the area, though none of them was bringing in any money. Sure, it was always a buzz to be able to drop into conversations phrases such as 'one of our properties' and 'our property portfolio' – John would even boast of this in his entry on the Friends Reunited website. As long as Anne had known him he had been rehearsing for eventual prosperity and his conversation was peppered with the self-congratulatory phrases of a far wealthier man. But while the 'portfolio' gave them kudos, the revenue they were seeking remained elusive. And with John working as a £25,000-a-year prison officer and Anne earning just £17,000 as a part-time doctor's receptionist, taking on a massive mortgage was out of the question.

But then they'd heard that two mid-terrace houses in Seaton Carew were up for sale: one as a family home and the other, already divided into bedsits, as an investment which, on paper, would generate an income of £2,000 per month.

'Just think, we get to live in an incredible house and earn money at the same time,' enthused John, but Anne, who had experienced many a sleepless night over the debts accruing on their other properties, wasn't convinced. Already they'd spent way beyond their means on their various houses and she had a sneaking suspicion they owed a huge amount of money on their vast collection of credit cards. John's new 'hobby' of playing the stock market during his free time didn't seem to be doing much to improve the situation and she wondered if there might be other debts that she herself wasn't aware of. Though Anne was an old-fashioned wife, happy to leave the finances up to her husband, even she was becoming increasingly uncomfortable with the fact that they had a serious problem.

Typical of John, once he knew about the two houses in Seaton Carew, he didn't let up, however.

'It's a once-in-a-lifetime opportunity,' he urged her, his small, hard eyes glinting like marbles in the sunlight. 'It's a potential goldmine. We could make a fortune.'

And that was John all over. Always thinking of the next big thing, the next big plan, without stopping to wonder how they might tie up the loose ends on the last scheme ... or even the one before that. They'd been married 27 years and when Anne looked back on the marriage it seemed a never-ending succession of plans, dreams and aspirations, each one overlapping with the last, all of them tailing off into nothing.

Of course she hadn't had a clue about any of that when she'd first set eyes on him on the school bus that took them from Blackhall Colliery to their respective schools in Hartlepool. Just 11 at the time, she didn't really pay much attention to the gawky, dark-haired boy with sticking-out ears. Not many people did, really. Even when, a few years later, he repeatedly tried to spark up a relationship with her, strolling self-consciously into the sweetshop next to his parents' home where she had a weekend job to lean awkwardly on the counter and make small talk over the sherbert lemons, she hadn't exactly been swept off her feet.

'Why won't you come out with me?' he'd ask, smoothing down his springy, untameable hair as if this might somehow make him suddenly irresistible.

Anne was flattered – after all, he was at college by this point while she was still attending school. But he wasn't really her type. There was something so intense about him, overbearing even. She was an attractive young woman, who'd already won the title of Miss Blackhall in a local beauty contest, and she could have her pick of the young locals, but John refused to let it lie. Every Sunday he'd be back, darting quick looks at her from those unsettlingly close-set eyes.

'Come on, come out with me, just one time. You won't regret it.'

And she'd given in, partly because she was a nice girl who didn't like to disappoint, partly because, with her sheltered convent upbringing, she was curious about what would happen, and in small part also because his single-minded persistence appealed to the vanity few people even knew existed in demure, devout Anne Catherine Stephenson.

She would quickly learn that when it came to dealing with John, acquiescence was definitely the path of least resistance. Not that she didn't have her own opinions on things, being steely determined herself when she set her mind to it. But in general she favoured an easy life, which meant more or less going along with what John wanted. Besides, after leaving school at seventeen, she always felt just a little bit, not inferior exactly, but perhaps less authoritative than her more educated beau. When Anne wanted to make her ideas felt she was more likely to do it through silences and sulks than talk or demands. And when she discovered John had briefly been engaged to another girl before they got together, her sense of being less worldly than him increased. Theirs was a relationship where, to adapt Orwell's phrase, both partners were equal but one was more equal than the other.

But all that remained still largely undiscovered territory when they exchanged wedding vows at St Joseph's RC Church in Blackhall on 22 December 1973. On that bitterly cold winter's day the guests had crammed into the tiny, low-built modern church, wearing heavy coats over their smart outfits. Nearly three decades on, Anne could still remember how nervous she'd felt walking down the aisle, just 21 years old, clutching her bouquet of red roses, with her father, Henry Stephenson, by her side.

Seeing John, 23, waiting for her at the top of the church, she'd been overcome with the blind excitement generated by the marriage of youth and love. For her it was certainly not a case of instant attraction, but over the four years that she and John had been courting she'd come to rely on him and to respond to his particular brand of humour, which veered sharply between lofty and coarse, leaving most people more baffled than amused.

Having been brought up in a family that took pride in living within its means, she was both thrilled and terrified by John's naked ambition. Despite the fact he was a primary-school student teacher while she worked as a printer's secretary, his conviction that somehow they would transcend their modest upbringing to enjoy the kind of lifestyle their parents could only dream of left her excited, but also slightly anxious. Would she be able to keep pace with all this upward mobility?

When the newlyweds bought their first home in Consett — in itself a slightly daring financial step — John typically insisted they kit it out with all the extra fittings, despite the fact that it was brand-new.

'Don't worry about the money,' he'd tell her when she held back about something, unsure whether they could really afford it. Often as not she'd end up feeling embarrassed about her fiscal prudence, seeing it through his eyes as vaguely provincial and petty.

'I'll be a millionaire one day,' John was forever telling people throughout the course of their long marriage. Something about his quiet, humourless confidence on the matter left others convinced he was probably right, although more than one must secretly have been unable to resist the hope that he would be proved wrong.

Over the years John always encouraged Anne to live way beyond their means, overstretching their finances, taking on more and bigger mortgages.

'You have to speculate to accumulate,' was his philosophy. Only by making big gestures, he felt, would they reap big rewards.

And yet here he was nearly 50 and, despite the personalised number plate and the bulging property portfolio, prosperity still seemed beyond his grasp. It was partly, Anne supposed, to do with the way he'd never really managed to stick at a career. When they'd married he'd been a trainee teacher and privately she'd often wondered how someone with such materialistic aspirations could have decided on so vocational a career. Almost from the start he'd found his profession frustrating. For eighteen years he taught science and maths to a succession of bored children who remembered him more for his unruly hair and the way he waved around his metre ruler than for any algebraic principles he might have drummed into them along the way. He was passionate about his subject, but somehow lacked the ability to connect with his young pupils. Nor was he known for his patience.

Eventually he became disillusioned with his chosen profession.

'There's no respect,' he'd complain to Anne. 'They're not interested in learning.'

Always slightly highly strung and often socially awkward, John found his interactions with unruly students and complaining parents increasingly stressful, plus, with two children of his own at home, he began to resent the long hours spent preparing for classes and filling in the piles of paperwork increasingly demanded by government guidelines. And so he began to look for another career that would allow him more time with his sons Mark and Anthony, born two years apart when he and Anne had been married just three years. Banking was the answer, he decided – a stable career with plenty of prospects for climbing the ladder. And yet, almost as soon as he'd joined Barclays Bank, he realised it was a mistake, for he felt hemmed in by the monotony of it all, each day apparently blending into the next with endless repetitiveness. And he loathed being told what to do. Truth be told, he had a tendency to feel superior to others around him, so taking orders from someone else was always hard, particularly when they requested that he do such tasks as selling financial products to clients who really didn't need them.

'I'm a trained professional,' he'd rant when he got home. 'Not a salesman.'

Just a year later he again changed tack. This time he had decided that it was the prison service that would fulfil his needs, providing flexible working hours which left him plenty of spare time to indulge his twin passions for outdoor sports and playing the stock market, a hobby he was secretly convinced would one day make him his fortune. He'd also have time to devote to building up a portfolio of buy-to-let properties that, he assured Anne, were a sure-fire way of generating cash.

'We'll be able to retire abroad,' he told her after they bought the first in a series of heavily mortgaged properties around County Durham, not altogether jokingly referred to by him as 'our pension'. 'Where do you fancy? Greece? Canada? The Caribbean?'

Moving abroad had long been a fantasy of John's. When he and Anne were first married he'd talked about Australia. Then Canada captured his imagination, followed by the Falklands... The world was their oyster, or so it seemed. He was always so restless, and as with everything else in his life it was always the one thing just out of reach that would make him happy, the place just beyond their grasp that might make him feel at home.

Yet somehow, once again things didn't work out exactly as he planned. He never quite fitted in with prison service life. His co-workers thought him a snob, always talking about how much money he had, or was going to have. And they were suspicious of the time he spent talking to the prisoners – he didn't seem to have much awareness of where the boundaries between staff and inmates lay, and that was something they regarded as highly dubious.

Financially too, it wasn't working out. Both John and Anne were working round the clock — at that time Anne had two part-time jobs, one as a doctor's receptionist and the other as a health service administrator. And then, in addition to their regular jobs, they were forced to attend to all the extra headaches that come with letting property — collecting rents, paying bills, arranging for repairs to be made, and so on. There were so many aspects of running a rentals business they hadn't considered. And yet still the wealth envisaged by John had never materialised. In fact, with all the properties heavily mortgaged and incurring crippling bank charges, while tenants paid late or not at all, they were becoming deeper and deeper in debt.

Anne didn't know the extent of the money they owed. As ever, John took care of the finances and she was more than happy to leave that side of their relationship to him. But she was made uneasily aware that their debts were mounting by the number of angry red bills that dropped through the letterbox (never pay a bill until the last possible day, was John's monetary strategy). And now here he was, talking her into buying yet more property, and the biggest financial gamble of their lives so far.

Convinced they were the way out of their current financial nightmare, John had a good feeling about the two houses in Seaton Carew. Sure, the £245,000 debt they'd have to take on was a worry, but they'd easily be able to manage it with the income generated from the bedsits — a few on the top floor of No. 3, the rest next door at No. 4.

'Just look at what we'd be getting,' he told Anne, warming to his theme as he gestured around them at the bleached sands, the golf course and the endless, fathomless sea. 'Isn't this what we've always dreamed of?'

Anne gazed over towards the pair of seafront villas and immediately imagined herself living in one of them – opening her curtains every morning to see the sun reflecting off the water, watching the trawlers drift serenely past, stepping out of the front door onto the beach... Wasn't that what everyone fantasised about? This could also be a new start for herself and John, she decided. Back home in Witton Gilbert she'd always made an effort to get on with the people living around them, but over the years John had somehow managed to alienate quite a few of their neighbours. One of those men who was nervous around people he didn't know well, he masked his awkwardness with arrogance or even hostility.

An intensely private man, he didn't encourage much contact with others except when he wanted to complain about something, such as the neighbour's lawn cuttings coming on to his property or a car being parked too close to his driveway. When another neighbour was having work done on his house and asked John, as a formality, if he could lean a ladder up against the wall, he was astonished to be refused permission. No, reflected Anne, John hadn't done much to make himself popular, but Seaton Carew was a chance to start again.

She knew the house was big, particularly now that Mark and Anthony had made their own lives down south after university. But they were always popping home to stay, and she could even turn one room into an office, where she could shut away the interminable paperwork from the rental properties she'd come to loathe. Perhaps John was right and this could be just the opportunity they needed. Thus Anne Darwin talked herself round to her husband's point of view, as she so often did, until the idea became so entrenched she almost took it for her own.

Still, Robert Meggs, the vendor selling the Seaton Carew houses, was puzzled when grey-haired, respectable-looking Mrs Darwin gazed at him on the day of the move, her large, slightly lugubrious eyes magnified by her spectacles, and announced flatly: 'If this doesn't work out, we'll lose everything.'

In some ways, living in Seaton Carew did change the Darwins' lives. Going to sleep each night to the sound of the waves crashing onto the beach outside their window was a thrill they never tired of, and John, who'd always been happiest outside doing something active, made the most of the opportunities afforded by living on the edge of the beach itself. As before, largely he kept himself to himself as far as the neighbours were concerned, but Anne was always ready with a smile and a friendly word, and she soon began to feel at home in their new surroundings.

But in a financial sense the move was a disaster for the couple. They'd overextended themselves in borrowing from the bank, plus they hadn't quite realised how much of a drain on their finances owning two enormous seafront houses might be. The salt-water spray and the relentless wind left the houses in constant need of repair and repainting. With this added to the upkeep demanded by rental bedsits, soon the overall costs were frighteningly high.

And when it came to the rent, people were just so slow to pay up. Increasingly there was some excuse, some reason to keep them waiting – their wages were late in coming that month, they'd had to lay out for car repairs, they were going to visit their daughter for a couple of weeks...

The mild-mannered, reserved, middle-aged Darwins were certainly no heavy-handed Rachmans. Unlike the notorious slum landlord of the 1950s, they weren't about to send a hired thug around when the rent became overdue but instead relied on polite notices and letters of reminder. And all the time the bank charges on their loans and mortgages climbed ever higher.

A few months after moving into No. 3 The Cliff, the couple were in big trouble. Bailiffs started to call round at the house they'd left in Witton Gilbert, while ominous-looking letters piled up on their former doorstep. Anne continued to work at the doctor's surgery in Durham, but any free time she might have had was taken up with dealing with the growing mountain of paperwork. The sound of the mail dropping through the letterbox filled her with dread – even the sight of their names in heavy black type on the official-looking envelopes was enough to give her that tightening feeling around her ribcage, as if the air was being slowly squeezed out of her.

Meanwhile John, never the most sociable of men, was growing ever more introspective. Though his elderly father lived down the road in Blackhall Colliery, County Durham, he rarely made the trip to visit him, let alone his one brother. In truth some family members privately believed he had ideas above his station and needed bringing down a peg or two. At his mother's funeral he hadn't allowed the sadness of the occasion to deter him from letting relatives know how well he was doing and how many houses he owned, even though, as his aunt Margaret Burns archly observed, they were 'colliery houses that they were practically giving away'.

Instead of socialising, he now spent hours on his own, outside kayaking or just walking with the dogs, or else holed up indoors on the computer.

'What do you do on there all the time?' Anne was constantly asking him.

She knew her husband still dabbled with the stock market, something that made her feel rather nervous given their current predicament. And she was also vaguely aware that he'd started playing one of those interminable Internet games that she herself could never quite fathom. Having brought up two sons, she wasn't exactly ignorant of all things technological, but fantasy war craft or role-play games remained a mystery to her. Still, at least it kept John occupied and took his mind off worrying about their increasingly precarious monetary situation.

But, with every day bringing fresh bills to pay, the couple could not ignore their mounting debt and putting forward ideas for a way out of penury became something of a dinner-table game between them.

'What if...?' one of them might begin.

'Supposing...' the other would continue.

And then there was one escape scenario that John persistently returned to, again and again: 'I could fake my own death.'

The first time he mentioned it, in the lounge at Seaton Carew,

Anne had treated the idea as a joke. Like everyone else in Britain of her generation, she'd been enthralled by the 1970s television comedy *The Rise and Fall of Reginald Perrin*, in which a harassed executive, played by the late Leonard Rossiter, sheds his old self and starts a new life, leaving his clothes piled up at the edge of the sea to make it look as if he's drowned. The idea of doing a Reggie Perrin as a way of solving domestic problems was commonly proffered in jest by people they knew and so when John remarked he'd be worth more dead than alive Anne laughed it off.

'Don't be so silly,' she told him dismissively.

But John kept on returning to the subject.

'We've got the £50,000 life insurance we had to take out when we bought this house,' he'd say to her, as if discussing a shopping bill, not his own prospective death. 'Then the mortgage on this place would be paid off if I was dead – that's another £130,000.'

As far as Anne was concerned, his fake death idea was on a par with 'If we won the Lottery...' conversations – a fantasy that made him feel momentarily better. But after a while she came to realise that he was more serious than she'd thought.

'It would solve everything, wouldn't it?' he insisted. 'You and I could go and live abroad somewhere, start a whole new life with no debts. We'd even have some money to invest once you'd sold these places.'

Then it would be up to Anne to come up with all the reasons why it was such a ridiculous plan.

'What about the boys, John?' she'd ask, trying to bring him back to earth. Mark and Anthony may be grown up but they were still a close family and she was sure that by bringing them into the picture she'd force him to think rationally.

'Oh, we'd figure something out,' was his evasive response.

Whenever she tried to offer up alternative courses of action, they'd be quickly shot down. Her suggestion that they should simply declare themselves bankrupt only made John purse his thin lips together in the dismissive way that he had.

'I won't end up living in a council house,' he snapped at her icily.

Each time they talked about the fake death plan, Anne thought that was the end of it. But then, a few days or even weeks later, he'd bring it up again.

Spring 2002 was the last time the couple discussed what Anne privately thought of as 'the Reggie Perrin plan'. By that point their financial situation was causing them both sleepless nights. Anne didn't know exactly how much they owed – to be honest, she didn't *want* to know, but she had an idea that it was in the tens of thousands. They had to come up with a proper scheme to rid themselves of some of their liabilities. And so when John began to talk again about different ways of 'disappearing', she wasn't exactly receptive.

'John, you're not thinking straight,' she snapped, eventually pushed to her limit. 'It's a crazy idea. Can we just talk about something else?'

She hated arguing with her husband and, by and large, their marriage had been marked by a notable lack of bust-ups. John wasn't the type of man to argue, but she could tell when he was angry because he became really quiet. She hated that quiet voice more than anything else; it was so ominous. Obviously, like any other couple they had their bad patches – times when she'd feel he wasn't paying her enough attention, or he'd let the frustrations of his job spill over into their life at home. But on the whole the last three decades had been fairly harmonious.

It wasn't that John was her dream partner any more, she supposed, than she was his. She'd never forget going into hospital in 1975 to have their first child, Mark. Her husband had been determined to be in attendance when their baby was born, but when, after a long and tiring labour, the Darwins were informed that Anne would have to have an emergency caesarian at which he clearly couldn't be present, he decided it wasn't worth staying on, she would later tell a spellbound courtroom. The feeling of abandonment she'd experienced when he left her in the hospital ward had stayed with her for years afterwards.

Similarly, in the late 1970s, when she'd discovered her husband had been having an affair, the devastating sense of betrayal and loss of trust had been hard to shake off. For a while she'd considered leaving him, but she couldn't imagine how she'd cope as a single mother. By that time she'd become used to functioning as part of a couple, to being in a partnership – even if more often she felt as if she was the junior partner – and she couldn't envisage life on her own again.

But the Darwins weathered those and other early storms, and after so many years together they'd come to fit around each other in a way that was comfortingly effortless. So close were they in fact that they hardly had other friends outside the marriage but relied solely on each other for support and companionship. True, Anne had her church choir while John had been a member of a gun club, but it hardly constituted a social life. John used to have a standing joke that the only time he ever took Anne out was to vote. Except it wasn't really a joke.

In lieu of friendships, Anne looked to John for entertainment. It was he who gave their lives excitement and adventure, continually striving for something more rather than being content to sit back complacently and let things wind down around them, like so many of their contemporaries were beginning to do. Although she was often worn out by him and his unrelenting schemes and his way of consulting with her but only really accepting her opinion when it matched his own, Anne recognised that he gave her momentum, while she in turn smoothed his more jagged edges.

Despite recent money worries, it had been a happy marriage on the whole, producing two wonderful sons who were her pride and joy. As a family they'd eaten meals together round the table, debating everything from what had happened at school to who was going to win the next election. Many times Anne had stayed at home preparing a meal for John and the boys to enjoy when they came back from sledging or biking, or whatever new adventure he'd planned for them. So close had they all been that when it came to choosing a university both boys had decided to study locally so they wouldn't have to leave home, Mark attending Sunderland University and Anthony going to New College, Durham.

Theirs had been a happy family, she now reflected. And if, as was happening now, John sometimes withdrew into himself slightly more than she'd like, well, she could accept that. Each of them had their own ways of coping with stress, and they'd always given each other space. In the end, she supposed, it was a couple's silences that said more about them than their exuberances – or rather, the quality of their silences. That she and John could coexist and understand each other without pressing for explanations or reassurances was, she felt, a sign of a solid relationship. Theirs was a silence of companionship, not misunderstanding fuelled by resentment and a sense of neglect.

And so when John stopped talking about the Reggie Perrin scheme and his face wore that distant, closed-off expression she'd come to recognise over the years, Anne didn't pay too much attention. Before long he'd come up with another plan, she was sure; he always did. Meantime they'd carry on rubbing along together as they always had. There was no need to make a big fuss, or to drag out of him what he was thinking; that wasn't how their relationship worked. Even when they were called in to see their bank manager in mid March 2002 and informed that the £245,000 loan they'd taken out to buy the Seaton Carew properties would have to switch from interest-only to repayment, causing their already crippling outgoings to skyrocket, John didn't spell out what was on his mind.

'Bankruptcy isn't an option,' he told Anne, his face closed to the possibility. And she, perhaps with some second sense of foreboding, didn't press him on exactly what, in that case, their options were.

And so she made what could be regarded as the most notable in a long series of big mistakes. For just as there are silences of complacency, so too is there the silence that accompanies complicity. John might have stopped talking about faking his own death, but that didn't mean he'd stopped thinking about it. And when Anne didn't bring the subject up again, he took this as a sign of taciturn approval, not complete dismissal. As far as he was concerned they'd discussed it, and now it was up to him to implement it.

All he needed was the right opportunity.

2
A GOOD DAY TO DIE

It was as good a day as any to become dead, reflected John Darwin as he held back the curtains, squinting into the pale morning light on 21 March 2002.

It was a Thursday, so far fewer people would be around than on a weekend, and the sea was nice and calm. No one would think twice about him getting into his kayak on a day like this. In fact it was just the situation kayakers love – still conditions, with a bit of a gentle breeze ruffling the surface of the water. He wouldn't attract any unwanted attention.

Now, it has to be said that normally John Darwin was a man who quite liked attention. His two cars – first, a luxury Jaguar and then a black Land Rover – each carried the personalised number plate B9 JRD and drew, or so he fondly imagined, considerable admiration. Two years after moving into the neighbourhood, he still experienced a little thrill from stepping up to the rather grand front door of his seafront home and putting his key in the lock, knowing holidaymakers on the beach were watching him with envy. In short, he liked to think that others regarded him as a man of some standing, the kind of man who attracted respect.

Except not today. Today he wanted to attract neither respect nor envy, nor indeed attention of any kind. Because today was the day he was going to disappear.

If there was a template for how a man about to fake his own death should behave, John Darwin wasn't aware of it. Which is probably why he got it so hopelessly wrong. In years to come he might wonder whether he should have made more of those last moments of his own identity. Should he, for example, have savoured the freedom of waking up in his own bed and throwing open the curtains without the worry of who might be watching? Maybe he should have lingered over coffee with Anne that morning, not knowing when he might see her again, or in what circumstances? Perhaps he ought to have relished the chance to enjoy the ordinariness of everyday conversation about work, the weather or the thousand and one other shifting topics that make up a marital dialogue.

In fact he did none of these things. As always, once an idea formed in his mind, he couldn't relax until he'd seen it through. Many times in the future he'd try to will himself back to that morning and urge himself to take a different path – or at least to think more clearly about what he was about to do. Look around you, he'd urge his former self, see what you'll be giving up, but no. As his parents, immediate family and teachers had come to learn over the years, once he had made up his mind about something there was no moving him.

So he didn't linger in his hallway later that morning before closing the door, or stop too long to ruffle the dogs' heads one last time. Instead his excitement and nerves propelled him across the beach, his kayak — which he'd romantically named *Orca* after the killer whale — under his arm, eyes fixed on the still, steady line of the horizon.

There would be no going back.

It would be fair to say that Holme House Prison in Stockton-on-Tees was not a happy ship in March 2002. Originally built for a maximum of 950, now the prison held a population that had swelled to over 1,000 and conditions were cramped and uncomfortable. Moreover, a shortage of staff meant that many inmates were confined to their cells for up to 19 hours a day. Unsurprisingly, tensions were running high. In fact, just a few months later, there would be a wave of violent protests by prisoners infuriated by their living conditions.

So, when John Darwin failed to show up for the night shift at 9.30pm on 21 March, his colleagues and bosses were far from happy.

Anne Darwin was in the bathroom when the phone rang. Typically, it had stopped by the time she reached it but by dialling 1471 she realised the prison had been on the line. With remarkably steady fingers she returned their call. No, she didn't know where John was. And no, she hadn't seen him all day, not since he'd gone out on the kayak early that morning. Yes, it was strange. No, she had no idea when he'd be back. And yes, she probably ought to report him missing to the police.

Replacing the receiver, she went over to the window. Whereas the sea had looked calm and benign earlier in the weak light of a spring day, now it was black and hostile and swollen with secrets.

Anyone looking at her from the outside would have seen a thoughtful, slightly apprehensive-looking middle-aged woman, watching for her errant husband, but the reality was completely different. For Anne Darwin was a woman in crisis.

Earlier that day she'd been at work when a call had come through from her husband.

'I'm about to do it,' he told her, his voice vibrating with excitement and fear. 'I'm going to take the canoe out.'

It hadn't taken long for the penny to drop. She felt a sudden lurch in her stomach, like when you start to pull out at a junction only to realise there's a car you haven't even noticed hurtling towards you.

'You can't do it today,' she began weakly. 'It's not good timing. Anthony's gone off to Canada with Louise and he's planning to propose. It'll ruin their holiday.'

But John was hardly listening. 'I'll need you to get home by 7pm so you can come straight back to pick me up from the car park at North Gare beach and take me to Durham station,' he told her. 'Don't let anyone see you.'

'But,' Anne protested weakly. 'But…'

Some days it seemed to her as if life with John had simply been a series of 'buts' all tailing off into nothing. Of course, she could just not turn up, she told herself through the remainder of that afternoon as she watched the clock in the medical centre slowly inch its way towards evening. She could refuse to have any part of it.

But she didn't.

Driving to North Gare, the northerly point of the mouth of the River Tees, about a mile from her home, as her hands rigidly clutched the steering wheel as if to keep her rooted to the seat, and to the here and now, she rehearsed what she'd say to John when she arrived. Clearly, the idea was nonsense, she'd tell him. People ran into financial difficulties all the time but they didn't go round pretending to be dead. There were other avenues they could take, other options to try...

But when, after she'd been sitting around in the deserted car park, he finally arrived, walking in jerky, self-conscious movements and dressed like the 'Milk Tray' man in jeans, black jacket, black hat and carrying a rucksack, she knew immediately from the set look of his jaw that there was no going back.

'I've done it,' he said, his eyes blazing with nervous energy. He went on to describe how he'd pushed off from the shore in front of their house earlier that day, heading south, and had then pulled in by North Gare pier further down, before pushing his beloved kayak back out to sea without him.

So, did Anne try to remonstrate with him, as she would later attempt to convince a courtroom she had? Did she list all the reasons why his crazy scheme was bound to end in disaster? Or did she, as was so often the case, become swept along by the sheer strength of her husband's convictions, until it was she who was envisaging the insurance cheques plopping through the letterbox and their new life abroad, untroubled by intimidating debt collectors or patronising letters from the bank?

Whatever, by the time she'd driven her husband the 40 minutes to the train station as instructed, already she knew he would not be dissuaded from his plan – which was to disappear off the radar for a few months, then come back when the insurance payments had already been made.

Later, at her trial, she attempted to paint a picture of a long-suffering wife who'd pleaded with her husband to listen to reason. 'I said: "Don't do it! Don't do it!"' she insisted from the witness box, staring intently ahead through her large glasses. But in the end, she maintained, she'd stood by him out of a mixture of love, loyalty and habit, plus fear of being left alone. She had no choice, she appealed to the jury. How else could she have kept her family together?

Perhaps it didn't seem to occur to her that helping John disappear without a trace, without informing their two sons of what was going on, might not be the best way to maintain a united family.

All through the drive home from the railway station the tears rolled down her face, although whether she was crying out of fear or despair, she couldn't really say. At the back of her mind danced a tantalising image of herself and John, debt-free at last, able to enjoy the things others take for granted such as opening the post without a sick feeling in the stomach, or paying by credit card without the fear that it might be rejected. And yet each time she tried to hold on to that image, the reality of her present situation came rushing to the foreground and she was overcome by the enormity of what John had put into action. A hard knot of nausea lodged in her throat. It couldn't really be happening, she told herself. Surely it wasn't real?

John had left strict instructions that she was to call the prison as soon as she got home, asking to speak to him as she would on any normal day. Then, when it was established that he wasn't there, she was to ring the police.

And yet, after walking through the front door into the suddenly oppressively silent house, she couldn't bring herself to pick up the phone. As long as she delayed making that call she remained a blameless, upstanding citizen, a devoted wife and mother, a good Catholic, a hard-working receptionist. One simple action would put her on the other side of the law, separated from her friends, her colleagues and her own children. However could she do that?

The longer she delayed carrying out his instructions, the easier it was for her to convince herself that it wasn't going to happen. Of course it wasn't really happening: she was no criminal, she'd never be able to carry off this ridiculous scam… She'd wait until John eventually rang and then she'd explain that she'd had second thoughts. She'd tell him to come right home and stop being so silly, she really would.

That's when she went into the bathroom and listened through the door to the ringing of the phone. When she came out and redialled the last number, she found herself telling her husband's sympathetic prison co-worker all about how he'd gone out in his kayak earlier that day and hadn't been seen since.

'Should I call the police for you?' he asked.

'No, no,' replied mild-mannered Mrs Darwin, just as a worried wife, anxious to set her own mind at rest, might do. 'I'll call them,' she insisted.

Which is exactly what she did. In the space of a few minutes, without really even stopping to think about it, Anne Darwin crossed the line from law-abider to law-breaker. Nothing in her life would ever be quite the same again.

For a while following her call to the police, no one knew what to think. John Darwin was a grown man – he could have gone off with friends, with another woman... Anything was possible.

When police came round to the house to collect more details, they found a nervous, agitated woman pacing about her first-floor drawing room, constantly darting glances through the window as though she might yet see her husband's kayak bobbing about in the dark North Sea. When the phone rang they thought nothing of it, naturally assuming it would be another shocked relative asking for news.

No one could possibly have guessed that when Anne Darwin excused herself to take the phone call in another room, the caller was none other than her own missing husband, eager for reassurance that his disappearance had been reported to the authorities.

'I don't think I can go through with this,' she hissed at him. 'Please come back.'

But he was delighted that the plan he'd been plotting out in his head for the past few weeks was finally taking hold. Always a man of action rather than words, the adrenalin coursing through him ever since he lifted his kayak from the hallway of their home that afternoon was keeping him curiously elated, even while he pondered how on earth he would manage to hide himself away for the next few weeks.

'You can do it,' he encouraged his wife. 'No going back now.'

Among the authorities and Anne's immediate circle of friends and neighbours there were those who privately doubted the missing kayak story. But when, in the early hours of the following morning, after a massive search operation, a battered double-ended kayaking paddle was found in the sea near North Gare, even the doubters began to have second thoughts.

As dawn broke over the North Sea Anne Darwin could see the coastguard and navy lifeboats scouring the water. A little later she heard a helicopter overhead and noticed a couple of larger navy vessels out at sea. She shivered in her big, draughty house, knowing what it meant: John's plan had been put into effect on a sickeningly grand scale; all the men out there were wasting public money and time searching for a man that she had herself dropped off at a train station just hours before.

She was in big trouble and it would only get worse.

Telling the family that John had gone missing was awful. His brother David had been supportive, but his father was elderly and frail, and of course took the news very badly. And then there were the boys. Somehow, even when John had first come up with the whole mad, crazy scheme, she'd managed not to think about that aspect of it all – that she'd have to cold-heartedly inform her sons that their father was missing, presumed dead and listen to their cries. In the end, luckily for her, she was spared that particular ordeal as close family members she'd gathered around her took the responsibility from her shoulders.

Mark was the first one to hear the news that would, in his own words, 'crush his world', when his uncle Michael, Anne's brother, phoned him in London (where he was working in IT) on 22 March to tell him his father had disappeared. Dropping everything, he raced north to be with his 'Mam', arriving in Seaton Carew after dark. Years later he would tell a rapt courtroom how, when he rushed up the stairs to the first-floor living room, his normally understated mother met him at the doorway and flung her arms around him, sobbing: 'He's gone, I think I've lost him!'

For the 27-year-old, his mother's uncharacteristically impassioned outburst of grief was almost as much of a shock to him as his father's apparent fate. But the truth was that by this stage Anne couldn't have stopped crying had she wanted to. True, the first tears had been born out of fear of what she'd started and the need to look convincing, but the longer the charade went on, the more it took on a life of its own. As more people were told, each one reacting with fresh shock and horror at the idea of John meeting some misfortune, alone and defenceless in the dark, forbidding North Sea, she'd become caught up in their emotion. It was as if their sorrow triggered off a well of sorrow deep within her, albeit more likely sorrow for herself and for the mess in which she'd allowed herself to become embroiled.

So, by the time Mark arrived, she had adapted to the part of grieving widow as if she'd been playing it all her life. Together they stood clasped in the doorway, the young man practically holding his mother up, and she allowed the tears to flow in a way she had rarely done in public. She wasn't crying for the stubborn, single-minded man in the woolly hat she'd dropped off at the station hours before, but for the family life that only now she was beginning to realise would never be the same again.

When he was finally able to tear himself away, Mark went over to the window, where he could see the flashing lights of the search helicopters hovering over the sea. Shuddering, he pulled the curtains shut, not wanting his poor mother to be confronted with the brutal evidence of his father's disappearance.

For two days, surrounded by friends, police officers and well-wishers, Anne and Mark kept up a vigil for John. During the daylight hours he strode up and down the seafront searching for clues, realising it was pointless but not knowing what else to do, while at night he begged his mother to eat, or held her as she wept.

Meanwhile the search continued. All that first day the search teams scoured the sea and land between Tees Bay and Staithes. As evening fell they were back out again after a strange object was sighted off the east Durham coast, but hope soon turned to disappointment when it was found to be two marker buoys in the area of an old outfall. After a second sleepless night, at first light they were out again, combing the area between North Gare and back towards Seaton Carew. Once again there was no sign of the missing kayaker.

John Darwin had simply vanished.

Mark would later describe to a newspaper how he held off phoning Anthony for as long as possible, hoping against hope that each phone call would be the one with news that would bring this whole nightmare to a close. But after John had been missing for two whole nights he knew he couldn't put it off any longer.

'I'll have to call Anthony,' he said gruffly, nauseous at the thought of it.

Barely perceptibly, Anne nodded, even though this was the part of the whole plan that had most bothered her from the very first time she'd realised what John intended to do.

'It seems such a shame to interrupt when he's going to propose,' she protested weakly, but Mark was adamant.

'He'd want to know,' he insisted.

But when the call was finally made to Anthony, on holiday in Canada with his girlfriend Louise, Mark's nerve failed him and it was left to his uncle to explain to his younger brother about their father's disappearance.

'I couldn't summon up the words to tell him my dad had gone missing,' he would later admit.

At first Anthony, then just 24, was unable to comprehend the seriousness of what he was being told. He would later describe to a Sunday newspaper how the phone call came at 7am when he was still half-asleep. Silly bugger, he thought to himself. He's been out on a canoe and got himself washed down the coast.

But when he woke up a bit more and thought about the reality of being lost in the North Sea for two nights, he realised just how grave the situation was. He'd been planning to propose at Niagara Falls, but instead he immediately cut short his holiday to return to his mother's side. Like his older brother, he'd enjoyed a close, loving relationship with their father, who, though often awkward with outsiders, had been the kind of dad you could always rely on for practical support – whether it was help with particularly tricky maths homework, or training for fun runs, or putting up a shelf or fixing a leaking toilet. They'd even joined in when he turned his hand to making and selling garden gnomes, helping him pour the concrete into the rubber moulds in the garage. And they'd enjoyed so many trips out together on bikes, or canoes or kayaks; it didn't seem credible that he could have paddled out to sea on a day when the water was calm as a reservoir, never to return.

None of it seemed real.

The Darwins were confused. Some witnesses said they'd seen John going into the sea very early the previous morning. But then someone else claimed to have spotted him around teatime, sitting in his kayak opposite The Cliff. Anne's anxiety increased with each new sighting, each potential witness. She wanted to get John back from wherever he'd gone, to fire questions at him, such as 'What are you doing?' 'What are you playing at?' 'What have you *done*?' And, most pressing of all, 'Why did you leave me to do this on my own?' But only the background humming of the helicopter and the relentless ticking of the clock were there.

While family and friends might have been willing to buy the lost-at-sea routine, others were not so easily convinced, however. Privately, members of Hartlepool Coastwatch and the local police who had expended so much of their time and budget mounting the £100,000-plus search, trawling tirelessly up and down the coast, craning for a glimpse of red fibreglass, wondered just how lost a competent kayaker could have got out on a sea that was, as they pointed out to one another, as still as a mill pond.

Up The Creek Without a Paddle

As the days passed, the search was scaled down and then stopped completely. Anne and her sons now entered a kind of limbo. It was as though she was a widow without actually being one. She had no husband, but neither did she have a body. People didn't know what to say to her when they saw her. Had John died in a normal way at least they'd have been able to choose from any one of a number of stock phrases designed to smooth over the awkwardness. 'He's in a better place now,' they could have told her, 'At least he didn't suffer,' and even, 'You'll carry him with you in your heart.'

But what do you say to a woman whose husband paddled off on a smooth-as-glass sea, yet neglected to paddle back again? Of course, you couldn't reassure her that he might be in a better place when there was still a faint chance that better place might well turn out to be Brazil with a stripper half his age, or staggering about the streets of London with a bandage round his head, not knowing who he was. It was so difficult.

In the weeks following John's disappearance, Anne felt a bit like a patient bravely enduring some terrible illness, while her nearest and dearest flapped about her, trying to make her more comfortable. True, much of the time she felt like a fraud, but she reluctantly grew used to being the centre of attention.

And in a way it made a change having the company in that huge, rattling house. It was ages since she'd had both her boys around her for such a lengthy period of time and, in any case, there's a limit to the human capacity for angst. Even in the darkest days, there were pockets of levity, when they'd all stand around in the kitchen with mugs of tea, sharing a family joke or a silly fragment of memory, even a comment on something completely unconnected with John.

A Good Day to Die

Those were the times when she'd convince herself that everything was going to be OK. In a few weeks' time John would come back with some credible explanation and everything would go back to how it was. Maybe they'd even turn it into a family joke one day – the day Dad went missing.

But if she sometimes managed to quell the background panic enough to start to enjoy the company of those closest to her, soon she'd be brought back to reality with a bang. Even while effectively dead, John just couldn't help wanting to run the show.

Time and again Anne would excuse herself from her concerned companions to take a call on her mobile only to find her errant husband on the line from the Lake District, where he'd been camping, demanding to know what was happening and when he could come back. He even made her take down the number of the nearest telephone kiosk, giving strict instructions on when she should ring.

John, it seemed, wasn't enjoying living hand to mouth in the solitary dreariness of a damp spring. He missed his home, particularly when he imagined Anne basking in the warmth of caring family and friends back there. It seemed strange that she was the one enjoying all the attention, when he was the one supposedly missing.

'It's not exactly easy for me either,' she would snap whenever he started to whine about how hard his 'disappearance' was turning out to be. 'How do you think it feels, having to lie to everyone the whole time?'

Each time he rang, John would be hoping against hope that Anne would tell him her support network had gone back to their everyday lives, leaving the coast clear for him to come home. He longed to be able to climb in between clean sheets, after a long, hot bath and fall asleep in his own familiar bed. Each time he would be disappointed.

The boys stayed with Anne for three weeks after their father's disappearance and did all they could to comfort their stricken mother. Even when they had to return to their own lives, they kept in touch by phone every day and travelled up to see her at the weekends. Privately they agreed that the feeling of being in limbo, of not knowing, was excruciating.

When the shattered remains of John's kayak were washed up six weeks after his disappearance, down the coast at Blue Lagoon Sands, near the entrance to the River Tees, Anne's more timorous acquaintances brightened up considerably. No longer did they have to dither around in uncertainty, not knowing if sympathy would be misplaced or premature. Here, at last, was a concrete indication that something bad had happened to him. Finally, the situation was moving into chartered waters, they agreed (without the least attempt at irony).

Still carried along on the wave of others' emotions, Anne began to ease herself tentatively into her new role as official widow. And to be fair, not all of it was play-acting. It was hard managing without John after so many years together. Like many long-standing couples, each had appropriated different but complementary roles over the years, so if one did the cooking the other washed up; one was the sensitive one, the other more lively. Now she was forced adapt to playing all these roles alone, and it wasn't easy. Even so, she couldn't help being irritated whenever John rang up, asking if he could come home. He always managed to sound so sorry for himself, as if it wasn't his own stupid fault that he was in this predicament. With each fresh call he sounded more desperate.

'I did this for us,' he kept reminding her whenever her anger got the better of her. 'So we wouldn't lose everything we've worked for.'

As her support network gradually peeled off one by one, back to the lives they'd put on hold the night John disappeared, the calls from her husband became increasingly urgent. 'I've got to come back,' he begged her. 'You don't know what it's like for me.'

The truth was, she didn't want to know. It was John's self-inflicted mess and he could clear it up all by himself, was her view. And yet you can't be married to someone for 30 years and not feel some of their pain. She knew he was living in a tent and had lost most of his money. Clearly, as a missing man he couldn't go to the ATM and withdraw any more cash, so he was more or less destitute. On wet nights she'd gaze out through the huge bay windows of the living room and wonder whether he had anywhere to shelter and how he was managing to dry his damp clothes. When the boys said something that made her smile, she felt a pang of regret on his behalf that he was missing out.

One day, weeks after his disappearance, when Anne was finally alone in her big, echoing house, John rang her in tears.

'You've got to let me come home,' he begged. 'Please, Anne. Please come and pick me up and bring me home.'

She hesitated. She was tempted to leave him just where he was to punish him for the mess he'd got her into, to force him to see exactly how it felt to have a partner who rode roughshod over your feelings and refused to listen to your point of view. But after three decades of marriage, old habits are hard to break. Besides, despite everything, she was missing her husband. Theirs was a traditional partnership where John was the man of the house, largely dictating what they did, and taking charge of all financial and practical matters. Physically, they'd remained close, enjoying the kind of flirty banter most of their married friends had long grown out of, and it made her feel, even at nearly 50, like a coy teenager. Without him around she felt lost and, now the boys had gone, rather lonely.

In the end she did what she'd always done – she went along with what John wanted.

3
DEAD MAN WALKING

The reunion between husband and wife near Whitehaven, Cumbria, did not, it's fair to say, resemble a scene straight out of *Casablanca*. For one thing, Anne Darwin was still seething with anger about what John had done, not to mention scared to death that someone might see them driving back together. Besides, he suddenly looked so old. For a long-married couple the Darwins still had quite a playful, frisky physical relationship, but the frail, stooped, bearded figure, leaning heavily on a walking stick, who was waiting for her at the designated meeting spot was a far cry from the virile, sports-fit man she'd dropped off just a few short weeks earlier. In fact, so shocking was the change that she didn't recognise him at first. She would describe to a reporter how she'd peered anxiously past the elderly man in his unfamiliar charity-shop clothes, in search of the John she remembered. If, in her weaker moments leading up to this point, she'd been envisaging a

Hollywood-style reunion, she certainly hadn't quite pictured her hero as Worzel Gummidge.

The drive home was a tense affair. Anne was tearful, fearful and purse-lipped. John, just grateful to be inside somewhere warm and dry, couldn't help but feel aggrieved at the way her disapproval pierced his euphoria, causing it to deflate slowly like a spent balloon.

'Everything I've done has been for us,' he said lamely, offering up his explanation like an inappropriate present.

But she simply clenched her hands tighter on the wheel, bit down on her bottom lip and drove on.

Back home at No. 3 The Cliff, John's buoyant spirits returned. A hot cup of tea, a warm, deep bath — it didn't take much to restore him to his usual single-minded self. He didn't mind admitting there were times over the past few weeks when he'd cursed himself for coming up with the fake death plan; times when he'd lain under dripping canvas, listening to the rain outside and the rumblings from his stomach, and wished he'd listened to Anne and declared bankruptcy. Unable to call on friends or family for advice or comfort, he'd been forced to turn inwards on himself, questioning his decisions, his motives, his judgement. As he luxuriated once more in the warmth of his family home, self-belief returned with a vengeance, though.

Of course he'd been right to preserve the legacy that he and Anne had worked so hard to build up for their children. And hadn't it all gone exactly as he'd envisaged? Except for one small matter: he wasn't really dead. And, as he was just learning to his dismay, the finance companies weren't about to pay out without a death certificate.

'I think it's normally seven years before a missing person can be legally declared dead,' people were forever telling Anne, as though having them spell it out for her would make the fact all the more easy to deal with. The problem was, they needed the money now. All the time John had been gone, the bills continued to mount up. With him effectively disappearing into thin air, there was no set protocol to follow as far as finances went. It was as if his affairs were suspended in time, freeze-framed, while the rest of the world carried on around him just as before. Bank charges still had to be paid, rents collected, mortgages kept up with...

Anne had already had all that explained to her. Barely a month after her husband's disappearance she asked Detective Constable Ian Burnham, the Family Liaison Officer assigned to her after John's disappearance, to call the Coroner to find out the protocol in cases such as hers and so she knew that when someone disappears their assets are legally frozen – that means no access to bank accounts and no disposal of their property. More to the point, no life insurance or pension policies could be claimed.

She'd heard all about Presumption of Death Orders, issued when someone is missing in suspicious circumstances, which allows their assets to be dealt with as with any normal death. Usually the courts only grant them after seven years and only if it can be proven that the person was exposed to a 'specific peril of death', although in exceptional circumstances this can be done earlier. But Anne and John knew they couldn't wait seven years. If John was legally dead Anne would be entitled to collect an amount from the prison service as well as pay off her mortgage and claim life insurance, but this was a deadly limbo, where nothing was being paid in but still everything continued to go out.

Anne was beside herself. At home the worries about money and what they'd done pressed in on her like a wet sponge. She and John could hardly be in the same room without an argument developing. Each time she looked through the windows of the house she was reminded of the lies she'd told and the predicament she was in; she had to get away. And so it was that, a few weeks after her husband's disappearance and with the minimum of fuss, she returned quietly to work in the doctor's surgery, keeping her troubles as tightly zipped as the comfortable cardies she liked to wear.

Patients at the Gilesgate Medical Centre in Durham, where she'd worked since 2000, would never have guessed from her calm, professional manner that here was a woman in the throes of personal crisis. As ever, she was welcoming and polite, unlike some of the doctor's receptionists you came across. Instead of getting impatient at people who came in wanting emergency appointments, she'd do her best to squeeze them in, never making them feel over-demanding.

Those who knew something of the calamity that had befallen her remarked to each other how well she seemed to be bearing up under the circumstances. According to her friend and colleague Irene Blakemore she'd been like that even when Irene had first gone to visit her at home, just a couple of weeks after John's disappearance. But then, as she pointed out, you wouldn't really expect anything else from Anne, would you? She was just that kind of person.

Dead Man Walking

At home, however, it was a different story. While John had been absent, Anne had started to familiarise herself for the first time with their finances. And the more she knew, the more furious she became.

'I can't believe you let us get into this mess!' she'd rant at John once he was settled back at home, out of sight of helpful friends and neighbours.

The desk in the office was piled with bills and tenancy agreements, plus official-looking letters that she couldn't bring herself to open, much less try to understand. She tried to get John to explain, but the figures seemed to swim fuzzily in the back of her mind before sinking slowly back under the surface of her consciousness, like a water-logged kayak. She knew they owed many thousands of pounds on the staggering 13 credit cards they'd somehow managed to amass, as high as £64,000 maybe more, but she couldn't bring herself to tot up the exact amount. Only one thing was certain: they badly needed the payout from John's death and they couldn't wait seven years for it.

'You have to have a memorial service,' people urged Anne, a lifelong devout Catholic, after it became clear that John was not going to be found. 'It will help you move on with your life.'

Consummate actress though she was becoming, she couldn't face the thought of a whole day of others' needless grief or their equally unnecessary sympathy.

'Poor thing,' they whispered. 'She still can't face the fact that he's gone.'

This was not precisely true. What Anne really was having trouble facing was the fact that John was very much present. And because of his idiotic plan there was absolutely nowhere else for him to be but present, in the house that was rapidly becoming more like a prison than a home.

John was a man who liked to be outside, keeping active. Incarcerated within the walls of his own house, even with its high ceilings and generous proportions, he felt as if the very bricks and mortar were pressing in on him. Whenever Anne had company, which to his easily irritated mind was far too often, he'd have to scuttle off through a hidden doorway in her bedroom to an empty bedsit next door in No. 4. This opening – a kind of coffin-shape, around five feet tall and eighteen inches wide – was disguised by a false-backed cupboard on either side, through which a person could easily slip unseen from one house to the other.

At the first sign of someone at the door, John would dive through the cupboard and emerge in a dingy room next door, where he'd hide out until the danger had passed – reading or playing games on the computer. Later on, of course, this would give rise to a whole rich vein of Narnia references in the tabloid papers, including the infamous *Sun* headline 'Liar, Witch and the Wardrobe'. But at the time public ridicule was the last thing on his mind.

John found being holed up in No. 4 particularly oppressive and would often stand with his ear pressed against the dividing wall, straining to hear what was going on in his marital home, feeling all the more keenly his own isolation and exile. The worst times were when the boys came to stay and he'd have to remain hidden away for days at a time, knowing all the while that just a few feet away were the sons he longed to see. Sometimes Anne would hear him pacing the floor in his self-created cell and again would come that stab of sympathy, laced with anger. She knew he was hurting, but it was his own fault.

Not surprisingly, she found she just couldn't relax. Not only was she worried the whole time that someone would come round unexpectedly, or that he'd be spotted through a window, but she also found being forced together with him 24/7 was putting an intolerable strain on her nerves. Like most couples, their relationship was largely structured around their separations. Going off to work, or for a run or a bike ride, provided each of them with a means of escape and a chance to recharge their batteries so that when they reconvened they'd do so having gained fresh perspective or at least new conversational material. But with John housebound, these separations became largely one-sided. While Anne was out seeing other people, breathing outside air, concentrating on something else for a change apart from them and their predicament, John remained at home like a hastily prepared stew, left to simmer all day in a pressure cooker.

She grew to dread walking through the door to find him waiting for her like a third dog, desperate to feed off whatever scraps of the outside world she was prepared to throw him. And more than that, she hated his new disguise. After his weeks in the wilderness he had come back sporting a look that could only kindly be described as 'David Bellamy meets Osama Bin Laden'. Secretly, she had been hoping this unfortunate new guise would wash off in the bath that first evening home, but instead he had embraced his new image, explaining to his slightly appalled wife that it was the perfect way for him to stay at the house in the knowledge that he wouldn't be recognised, and also for him to implement Step Two in his master plan, which was to assume a new identity.

Now that John had realised the fake death scam was going to take longer than he had initially thought, he quickly worked out that if he wanted to have any kind of a life while in hiding, he'd need to reinvent himself. He'd heard about people looking through graveyards and obituaries to steal the identity of anyone roughly the same age who'd been dead for some time. Like many people of his generation, he'd seen the film *The Day of the Jackal*, in which the lead character, an assassin, adopts the identity of a dead child as part of his murder plot. To that end he decided to appropriate the name of John Jones, a baby who'd died in 1950, shortly before he himself was born, and who was buried in a Sunderland graveyard. The ever-resourceful John found out the details in a local paper. His ultimate goal was a passport in the name of this new fictitious persona, but he decided to start small – with a library card. He knew that a vital part of the passport application was to get a photo signed by someone in authority who'd known you for two years or more. Who better than a local librarian?

He was understandably nervous the first few times he decided to leave the house in his precarious new guise, not least because of the possibility of bumping into his own frail father, who had taken to patrolling the coastline and gazing out to sea in search of his missing son. Never one to downplay anything, John accessorised his longer hair and beard with that same woolly hat, of which he'd grown rather fond, plus a plaid shirt, walking stick and a pronounced limp.

If he'd been let loose in the dressing-up box of an amateur

dramatics society he couldn't have put together a more attention-grabbing ensemble. Yet strangely, he seemed to think this bizarre garb rendered him if not invisible, at least anonymous. Residents of Seaton Carew would later distinctly recall seeing the odd-looking figure limping up and down the beach, but for some reason John felt his new disguise enabled him to blend seamlessly into the background.

But from Anne's point of view the problem was that having your toned, fit husband turn overnight into a hillbilly Captain Birdseye was not exactly helping to thaw out their frozen relationship. By this stage she was living in a state of perpetual nervous agitation. Anything was enough to startle her – the ringing of a phone, a shout from outside – and so catching sight of this strange bearded man in her kitchen out of the corner of her eye was often enough to bring on a sudden blinding panic, followed by a crushing feeling of resentment and regret.

The only release from her relentless anxiety was sleep, but always in the morning would come the agonising moment when she'd be jolted out of the blissful serenity of the night to the sudden realisation of what she'd done and who she was now. Anne Darwin, née Stephenson: liar – and if she carried along on the path she was on, soon-to-be criminal.

Throughout her life convent-educated Anne had done everything by the rules. Growing up in Blackhall Colliery, the apple of her parents' eye, she'd been known around her neighbourhood for her friendly disposition and her willingness to help others. She'd never, as her family were fond of saying, caused them a moment's bother. As she'd grown older that cheerful conformity had never left her. She'd married young and well, raised her boys in an exemplary way, and apart from the financial chaos of recent years, she continued to run her life as though according to a textbook.

But now everything had changed. Suddenly she found herself looking over her shoulder as she went in and out of her own house. She no longer opened the curtains without first checking there was nothing to 'give the game away' and her heart lurched with every knock on the door. From being a friendly, affable woman, she now lived in dread of people inviting themselves round, or worse still, calling in unexpectedly. Every unfamiliar car that drew up outside was a threat, every stranger across the road a potential informer.

She no longer remembered what it felt like to leave the front door wide open when she went out to empty her rubbish, or to talk to her sons without feeling her heart constricting. Anne Darwin, the girl who'd never put a foot wrong, now lived in constant fear of being exposed as a fraud. Frequently, especially after one of the boys had rung to tell her about an unidentified body that had been found somewhere, or how much they were missing their father, she would threaten to call the whole thing off.

'You can't back out now,' John would warn her. 'You're the one who reported me missing! You'd be in big trouble. And what about the cost of the search? We'd have to pay that back, as well as all our other debts.'

Anne would try to disregard him. She imagined going to the phone and calling up either of her sons. 'Your father's alive,' she'd tell them. 'He's back home with me.' But then, in her imagination, she never got past that point. What could she say to her boys after that? That together their parents had plotted to deceive them, that she'd watched them grieve, knowing she could bring their suffering to an end with just a few words, but had kept silent? That their parents had been facing bankruptcy and so were in the process of engineering a major fraud to get out of it; or that although she'd always taught them to do the right thing, she herself was doing the wrong thing every moment of every day? How could she tell them the truth when that truth was so multi-layered and difficult to unravel?

And so she said nothing.

While her feelings of anxiety never quite went away, with each passing day she began to feel slightly more comfortable in her role and to wear her widow's weeds, if not with abandonment, at least with a certain air of authority. Still in shock from the bomb that had blasted through her family on the day John decided to go 'missing', she didn't find grief too hard an act to put on and indeed, at times, she played the part to such perfection she surprised even herself.

In August 2002, when a body was washed up off Hartlepool, DC Ian Burnham, the officer assigned to her case, called to break the news and to ask her if she wanted to come in and identify the body. But Anne didn't have time to digest this new bombshell, let alone think how she'd be able to deal with it, before he was back on the phone again.

'I'm so sorry,' he told her, unsure whether his news would be good or bad. 'The body has been confirmed as someone else.'

At this she burst into tears of relief, which she soon disguised as grief. 'I so wanted it to be John,' she sobbed. 'I just want him to be laid to rest so I can move on.'

DC Burnham felt moved by the dignified anguish of this very self-contained, brave woman. It was only natural she'd want a body to mourn. He could only guess how she must be feeling.

But no one could really know how Anne Darwin was feeling. And those who tried would later discover how wide of the mark they really were.

Six months on from John's disappearance, Anne again had a chance to demonstrate her acting prowess when she appealed for help in finding her husband.

'People die, have a funeral, have a headstone. There is something to mark the fact that they existed on this earth, but without a body I don't know how we can mark John's life,' she told the handful of reporters who continued to show a vague interest in the case. 'All I want is to bury his body; it would enable me to move on. It's difficult to grieve without bringing things to a close, but as it is I'm in limbo and there's nothing I can do.'

Ever dignified, she spoke movingly about how the sound of the waves crashing outside the window on the shore brought the memories flooding back. 'The view from my window is a daily reminder,' she said. 'This was to be the house of our dreams. I have got to look out and not dwell on the tragedy.'

Then the doctor's receptionist with the neat, grey bob and rimless glasses said something that, had anyone been paying attention, might have sounded a little, well, odd: 'I have no reason to think he would have left and stage-managed this.'

And so 2002, the year the Darwins' world fell apart, passed slowly from summer to autumn and then on to winter. Christmas was a particularly difficult time, with John forced to spend long periods confined next door while Mark and Anthony or other concerned family members made sure Anne's first Christmas as a widow passed as painlessly as possible.

On one occasion the boys were shocked to find their father's angina medicine still in a cupboard in the kitchen. 'Mum, isn't it about time you got rid of some of Dad's stuff?' they asked gently, then were mortified by the startled, almost frightened look in their mother's eyes. The following day the medicine had disappeared.

As the months wore on, pressure to settle the Darwins' financial crisis mounted. Under John's guidance Anne managed to get her debts frozen so they stopped accumulating interest, but she still didn't have a way of paying them off. She, or rather John, started writing off to the authorities to explain her situation and to ask how one went about having someone declared dead. Confined to the house and going out of his mind with boredom, the normally physically active John threw himself into his new job as director of correspondence and scanned Anne's signature into the computer so that he could rattle off letters in her name.

There would need to be an inquest, they discovered, where it would have to be proven there was sufficient evidence to demonstrate John was dead. Only then could Anne go about securing her position as a legal widow to get the insurance payouts they were relying on. Of course it was also explained to her what would happen in the unlikely event that a death certificate was granted by the Coroner and the person was later found to be alive. Surprisingly, one might think, if the beneficiary made their petition in good faith, it was just possible they might not have to pay the money back.

Each request for an inquest in the case of a missing person – of which there are only a handful each year – has to be sanctioned by the Home Secretary, at that time David Blunkett. To the surprise of many, Anne's request to speed through an inquest was accepted and a date set for April 2003, just over a year after John's disappearance.

'It'll be such a relief,' she confided in her friends and family. 'Finally I'll get some closure.'

The American expression, so beloved of Californian psychotherapists, sounded strange coming from this proper, very English woman, but everyone knew what she was trying to say. And indeed closure was thought to be an eminently sensible thing to desire, given the circumstances.

The setting of a date for the inquest finally gave Anne the impetus to start thinking about a memorial to coincide with the anniversary of John's disappearance.

'What about a bench with his name on it?' she suggested to her sons. 'We could put it on the seafront facing out to sea.'

But Mark was worried about it getting vandalised. Instead the widow and her sons agreed on a more intimate commemoration. On 21 March 2003 all three ventured out into the chill spring air and made their way across the beach to the right of the house, to Seaton Carew pier. At the end, with the wind blasting through their winter jackets, they threw three carefully prepared wreaths of flowers out into the sea.

'That poor woman,' neighbours whispered when they saw what was happening. 'If only he could see how much he was loved.'

But of course John knew only too well. From his hideaway at No. 4, he could just about spot the sorry little band at the end of the pier.

Irene Blakemore was moved to discover that her friend Anne, who always kept her sorrow so tightly wrapped, had detached one bloom from her wreath and slept with it by her bed. Whether Irene would have been quite so touched had she known Anne was sharing that bed with the very man whose death she was commemorating is up for debate, but what the incident showed was that Anne Darwin, the modest, silver-haired doctor's receptionist who'd always been so under the influence of her domineering husband, was finally getting into her stride.

Over at Holme House Prison, where John had worked for years but failed to win many friends, gaining a reputation for being slightly aloof as if he felt the job to be beneath him, the buzz going around on the anniversary of his disappearance was less charitable.

'He's done a bunk, crafty beggar!' his colleagues agreed, their voices tinged with reluctant admiration.

Still, no one was denying his wife the right to grieve. After all, in the end she had been left alone to face the music and to pick up the pieces of the so-called 'dream' life they'd planned together. She deserved her closure, and good luck to her.

With an inquest date fixed she slowly began, at least as far as appearances went, to rebuild her shattered life – accepting invitations out with friends who'd secretly always found John hard work, forming new bonds with other 'single' women in her social circle. And if, on some occasions, she seemed a little preoccupied and tense, well, that was only to be expected.

Grief, her newly discovered friends kept telling her, did not follow a neatly defined linear path, but was flabby and uncontained, seeping out at the edges, impossible to pigeonhole. Anne would get used to it, they assured her, using that favourite phrase of mourners-in-waiting: time is a great healer. John, they told her kindly, wouldn't want her to stand still, but to get on with her life. And never forget, he'd always be with her.

Anne, her huge soulful eyes magnified by a blur of tears, would sniff and nod obediently.

Yes, John would always be with her.

That was the problem.

Right up until the day of the inquest, 10 April 2003, Anne Darwin refused to believe it was actually going to happen. For months John had been pushing for it, but she'd been trying not to think about it, convinced something would crop up beforehand that would allow the whole thing to be called off – she'd inform the authorities, he might be spotted.

There was absolutely no way, she told herself, that she could sit through an inquest into her own husband's disappearance, knowing all the time that he was pottering around back at home. She was not that kind of woman. And yet, on the appointed day, she got up as usual, dressed in her smartest clothes, ran a brush through her grey hair – hopeless to try to coax any body out of it, she'd learned years before – and got ready to meet Mark and Anthony at Hartlepool County Court for all the world as if she really was a grieving widow, desperate for 'closure', just as she'd said.

Slowly mounting the steps of Hartlepool Law Courts, an imposing modern red brick building which houses both the County Court and the Magistrates Court and practically backs on to the police station, she couldn't help but be impressed by the sheer magnitude of the place. A building like that carried real gravitas, she felt. She could have little idea how well she'd come to know these labyrinthine corridors in years to come, nor how much she would begin to dread the sight of those sheer brick walls.

What must it have been like for upstanding, prim Anne Darwin to sit through that inquest, her heartbroken sons at her side, listening to Coroner Malcolm Donnelly talking about John as if he might really be dead, just hours after he'd seen her off with a peck on the cheek in the rudest of health? How on earth did she manage to keep herself from leaping to her feet to halt proceedings, turning to the gathered onlookers to say, 'There's been a mistake'?

Whatever the struggle that might be going on inside her, she gave nothing away.

'She's so brave,' people kept saying, seeing her gravely determined expression.

The Coroner decided that as the original police investigation had found no suspicious circumstances, no evidence to think it might have been suicide, and there was no body, there were sufficient grounds to consider the fact of death to be probable and to return an open verdict. In other words, as far as the law went, John was, to all intents and purposes, a goner.

As he'd gone missing at sea the death certificate would be issued by the Marine and Coastguard Agency Registry of Shipping and Seamen, but following the inquest, this was just a formality.

Leaving the court, Anne and her sons came across John's father Ronald, who insisted he'd been told the wrong time and had turned up an hour and a half late. Naturally, the old man was agitated to have missed the proceedings. In fact, he hadn't wanted the inquest to take place at all, considering it to be almost a betrayal of John to rush through a declaration of death when no body had been found. But then, as everyone else said, Anne needed to get on with her life and this was just another thing that she had to do in order to move forward.

After the inquest Mark and Anthony accompanied their mother back to the house in Seaton Carew. As they let themselves in one of the dogs came towards them, wagging its tail with excitement. It was carrying something in its mouth, something soft and faded and rather shabby-looking.

'Oh, it's John's slipper,' Anne said, and no one needed to pass comment on the symbolism of the moment.

For once, neither of the two boys felt compelled to ask their mother how long she planned to keep their father's clothes and shoes preserved upstairs, just as he'd left them the day he'd gone out to sea, a little over a year before.

Anthony and Mark were in sombre mood as they tried to make sense of the somewhat surreal proceedings they'd just witnessed. It was, after all, their father's life (or death) that had been under discussion, and yet it had seemed at times so impersonal it hardly seemed possible that it involved them at all. What's more, their mother seemed unusually tense, but then how else was she supposed to act? If there was a protocol for a woman waiting for a court official to tell her whether she's a wife or a widow, the Darwins didn't know of it.

Back at No. 3 The Cliff, the house that had never really been home to the Darwin sons, who had moved on themselves before their parents relocated there, Anne seemed fidgety and unable to relax. Not that surprising, they supposed, in view of what had just taken place.

'At least you can move on now,' they told her, lamely reiterating what she already knew in a clumsy attempt at providing comfort.

But she seemed to be hardly listening. 'Yes,' she nodded vaguely, her eyes constantly darting around the room, to the door and then back again. 'You're absolutely right.'

Finally, when both boys were long gone she signalled to John that the coast was clear. When he eventually emerged from next door she had to stifle an almost hysterical giggle. Here was her now officially deceased husband, popping out of a cupboard in her bedroom. What kind of a life was she leading where such a thing could be conceivable? How had she, who'd never put a foot out of line, ended up in this situation?

'Congratulations,' she told him dryly. 'You're dead.'

John smiled, a rare enough occurrence since he'd been back. Finally it looked like his plan, his act of sacrifice, was about to pay off. Now that he was dead Anne could claim on the insurance, as well as any fund she might be due from the prison service. She'd be able to pay off the mortgage on their houses, then sell them off and pocket the cash. It would take time, but it wasn't as if she had any reason to hurry.

'The boys were really upset,' she told him, perhaps only now realising the full cruelty of allowing her sons to sit in the family home and grieve for their father, while all the time he was sitting next door, probably playing mindless fantasy games on the computer. What kind of a mother was she?

'A loving one,' John reassured her. 'A mother who wants to make sure her sons have a decent inheritance, rather than be saddled with debt.'

But still, as she lay in bed that night unable to sleep, she kept thinking about her boys, going through their lives fatherless, always with the feeling that something was missing. Was the money really worth their sorrow? Would they ever forgive her, should they find out?

For his part John drifted almost effortlessly into unconsciousness, perhaps exhausted by the excitement of the day and the coroner's verdict, with all that it implied. He might almost be said, thought Anne, looking at his peaceful face in the semi-darkness, to be sleeping the Sleep of the Dead.

4
THE GHOST IN THE CUPBOARD

In many ways being officially dead was a great improvement on being wishy-washy *un*dead, John decided. At least now he had a status, and bizarrely that seemed to make him feel more concrete and tangible.

Yet, in real terms, he was in effect a ghost. And that was a more complicated reality than he had first anticipated. For a start, he could hardly go out. While he'd been on enforced 'leave of absence' in the Lake District following his disappearance, he'd enjoyed an anonymity he now coveted nostalgically, conveniently forgetting how homesick he'd once been. But now he was back in Seaton Carew going out was fraught with danger. There were just too many risks of being spotted by people who knew who he was, or rather, who he *wasn't* any more.

On the bleakest of winter days this wasn't such a problem. Then the beaches were largely deserted and he could take long, bracing walks buffeted by the cold northerly winds, secure in the knowledge that few locals would think this a good day for a stroll. Turning his face towards the sea, he'd breathe in the fresh, salty air and hold it in his lungs, as if trying to capture the very essence of freedom.

But on other days, when the beaches were dotted with mothers and shell-collecting toddlers, not to mention newly retired couples in matching exercise outfits power-walking along the promenade, he was confined to his house, or worse still, to the bedsit next door.

As the summer — or what passes for summer in those parts — slowly edged its way across the sands of Seaton Carew, John Darwin could only stand at the window and gaze out at the increasingly populated beach. For a man who prided himself on his fitness and felt stifled if he spent too long indoors, this was a kind of torture, watching other men launch themselves off from the shore in dinghies and kayaks, knowing he couldn't just throw on a pair of shorts and go out there to join them.

He spent hours reading every book he could lay his hands on — novels, history, world atlases, anything that gave him a momentary glimpse of the world outside his seafront prison. And when he wasn't reading he was on the computer, losing himself in fantasy role-play games where he could act out all the scenarios closed off to him in real life. At a click of a mouse he could roam continents, sail seas, fly off to different galaxies. He could be hero, saviour, villain or defender. Hiding behind his chosen moniker, he could interact with other game-players with a freedom he had lost for ever in the real world, if indeed he ever had it.

The Ghost in the Cupboard

His favourite game was reportedly EverQuest, the massively popular online role-playing game inspired by Dungeons and Dragons. Players select a character (or an atavar) and assign to their character an adventuring occupation such as wizard or cleric. As their characters they explore a fantasy world, fight monsters and enemies for treasure and points, and trade skills with one another, progressing through various levels. John was a druid, a member of the priest-class, able to cast powerful spells to heal and to destroy, and perhaps most poignantly for him, to teleport to different zones and dimensions.

For those drawn into the fantasy world of computer games, gaming can prove dangerously addictive. Suicide, marital breakdown and child neglect have all been blamed on game playing pursued to the exclusion of almost anything else.

A key element of many of the fantasy-style computer games is joining up with other players for role-play or combat. Players can group together to go adventuring, staying in their groups for extended periods of time, cyber-chatting sometimes for hours on end, day after day, with the result that quite intense friendships are formed relatively quickly.

In the absence of a social or work life beyond his wife, these online attachments assumed disproportionate importance for John. They were his link to an ordinary world, where people exchanged inane chat, idly commented on items in the news, joked together and asked after the weather in their respective hometowns. To the many people who knew him only as John the Druid, he could be anything he wanted to be – teacher, mystic, wanderer, nomad... He could weave for himself a fantasy life as rich as the imaginary cyber world on his computer screen, but when he finally pressed the 'off' button and the images faded to nothing, taking with them his network of unseen internet 'friends', the silence seemed unbearable. Suddenly the room, minutes before a gateway to another galaxy, revealed itself as just a space, its four walls oppressive in their dull solidity, the paint chipped, the carpet worn.

It was at times like this that he felt the reduction of his circumstances most keenly, the way his life had become so diminished as to fit neatly into one medium-sized room. For the first time he really appreciated what the men he'd been in charge of at Holme House Prison had felt when they listened to the key turning in the lock, the metallic echo of a hundred cell doors slamming in sequence. Never the most empathetic of men, he now understood at least a fraction of how it must feel to be locked up in a cell 19 hours a day, measuring out your world in a handful of paces, your only connection to the outside the changing quality of light in the patch of sky through your cell window.

Very occasionally, the feelings of claustrophobia would be too much and he'd be driven to take an uncharacteristic risk, but two separate incidents convinced him that he had to lie low.

Once he was going down the somewhat shabby stairs of No. 4 when, too late, he realised someone else was coming up and Lee Wadrop, one of the bedsit tenants, came into view. It was too late for John to hide, and one glance at the look of sudden recognition in the other man's eyes was enough to tell him there would be no point in attempting to be someone else.

The Ghost in the Cupboard

'Aren't you supposed to be dead?' asked Lee, gazing at him in mild bemusement.

John tensed all over, too shocked by the sudden turn of events to come up with a plausible story to explain away his appearance. So shocked, in fact, that he blurted out the first thing that came to mind: 'Don't tell anyone about this.'

For a few seconds that seemed to John to last a lifetime, the two men stared at each other, but then Lee shrugged as if this was none of his concern and brushed past him, continuing up the stairs, his interest already transferred to something else. Though John walked on the most fragile of eggshells for the rest of that week, it soon became obvious that his luck had held. Lee wasn't about to alert anyone to his sudden reappearance.

'I didn't want to get involved,' Lee Wadrop would later explain.

In that, the Darwins were lucky. Generally the bedsit tenants were a very private lot, who didn't pry into anyone else's business so long as they were left alone. It had been a very close call, however.

The second incident came when a former prison colleague spotted John with Anne.

'I saw John,' the man insisted. 'I *know* it was him.'

Anne didn't hesitate. 'You must be talking about his cousin who was visiting,' she told him smoothly. 'There's a strong family resemblance, isn't there?'

In both cases there was no follow-up from the sightings, no anonymous tip-offs, no rumours were spread, but they caused enough sleepless nights for John to accept that he had to remain indoors, no matter how stifled he might feel. It was a bitter lesson to learn.

Up The Creek Without a Paddle

While her husband was adjusting to the limitations of life as a dead man, Anne was also doing some major rethinking herself. Having spent most of her married life his shadow, believing she'd never be able to cope on her own, suddenly she was the more powerful partner in the relationship, at least in real, everyday terms. She had access to money, she went out to work, she socialised with friends... He merely sat, and waited. Unable to go out, Anne became John's single link to the outside world and it was a fairly onerous responsibility. Not since the boys were small had she felt such a sense of being required, of being so essential to someone else's well-being. And it was more than a bit irksome.

No sooner did he hear her key in the door than he was scurrying down the staircase, desperate for some company after a day spent pacing the floors of the draughty house.

'What happened at work today?' he'd quiz her as she sank down exhausted on to the sofa, not wanting to do anything but flop. She knew he was desperate to experience second-hand through her the life to which he no longer had access and she tried not to become irritated by his need for her attention, but she couldn't help feeling, well, encroached upon. She was used to having her own space, but now she felt constantly invaded, like when someone sits too close to you on the bus.

'It won't be for long,' he would say whenever she got frustrated with the situation. 'Just until the money comes through.'

When that wasn't enough to placate her he'd use the other fallback line that sometimes guilt-tripped her into silence: 'I did it for us.'

Sometimes, however, Anne refused to feel guilty. Those were the times when she allowed herself the indulgence of a new, largely unfamiliar emotion – anger. She had always thought of herself as the peacemaker, the one who tried to smooth over John's rougher edges, but now she found she was constantly trying to keep a low-level resentment under control. Every now and then she gave up and her accumulated rage came gushing to the surface in a torrent of abuse and accusation.

'What gave you the right to put us in this situation?'

'How could you be so selfish?'

The rows were bitter and heated, and occasionally John would end up flouncing off to his bedsit next door, the dramatic effect of his exit somewhat diminished by his having to first climb through a cupboard to do so. Sometimes Anne would be so enraged she'd bolt the adjoining door behind him, effectively sealing him off in his bedsit – unless he wanted to risk the main stairs of No. 4. Still shaking with indignation, she'd lie in bed, aware he was probably doing just the same on the other side of the wall.

The ongoing resentment made having a physical relationship almost impossible – as Anne would later divulge in press interviews. Many women can't relax in the bedroom if there are things niggling them outside of it. While men tend to be skilled at compartmentalising, able to ditch everyday grudges at the bedroom door and concentrate on the job in hand, women often find that if they're fed up with their partner not pulling his weight around the house, or angry about an unpaid bill or a careless remark, intimacy is the last thing on their minds.

So it was with Anne. After all John had put her through, all he continued to put her through, she simply didn't feel like being physically close to him. Plus, secretly, she found the David Bellamy disguise he'd become so fond of more than a slight turn-off.

The worst times for her were when the boys came to visit. Most of the time she could join John in looking on what they were doing as a bit of financial one-upmanship. The insurance companies were massive and the sums they would be paying out were just small change to them. But when her sons were around she would be struck once more by the human cost of the whole sorry enterprise.

'How can you sit in that room, knowing your own sons are next door, still grieving because they think you're dead?' she'd ask him when he emerged tentatively from the cupboard after a visit from Mark or Anthony. 'What kind of a father are you?'

But, of course, what really bothered her was what kind of mother *she* was. What kind of mother could see her children in pain, knowing she had the means to end it and not do so?

The worst occasion was Anthony's wedding in September 2003. Anne knew how much her younger son would have wanted to have his father present when he married Louise. When the bride's father made a toast to absent friends she could see from his expression exactly who his thoughts were with. Yet still she said nothing, returning to Seaton Carew full of self-loathing and doubt.

John usually tried to be patient whenever she got into one of these states, once again talking her through what was to him perfectly obvious.

'If you told them you'd just be replacing one kind of pain for another,' he explained for the millionth time. 'How could you explain to them what we've done? How could you bear them to have to watch you going bankrupt, or me going to prison? You wouldn't be sparing them anything, Anne.'

And so she'd remain silent whenever Mark or Anthony brought up the subject of their father. Or she'd be deliberately vague. She found one phrase particularly useful in this respect.

'How are you, Mam?'

'Oh, you know…'

'Are you getting used to living on your own?'

'Oh, you know…'

It wasn't lying, she reasoned to herself, just not being entirely specific.

At least she was able to reassure the boys when it came to the subject of finance. In fact they were pleasantly surprised by how very on-the-ball she seemed to be about putting in motion all the paperwork for claiming insurance and death-in-service payments now that John was officially, on balance of probability, dead. Considering their father had always taken charge of most of the financial affairs, Mam seemed to be dealing with all the complicated legal stuff with remarkable ease.

In addition to the life insurances – one of £25,000 and the other, attached to the mortgage, of £137,000 – John's long career as a teacher entitled her to around £84,000 from two pension schemes – one a teachers' and the other a civil servants' – and two smaller amounts of £2,000 and £2,273 from the Department for Work and Pensions. It was an impressive amount of money, but the paperwork involved in claiming it already accounted for the destruction of several square miles of Brazilian rainforest. Anne, however, didn't seem to be fazed. 'Well, it helps give me something to focus my mind on,' she said lamely when one of her sons brought up the subject of her newfound efficiency.

The boys were relieved. Given what had happened, she could so easily have gone to pieces, moping around the over-large house and not knowing what to do with her life. But instead she was thinking of the future, making sure she had the money she was entitled to, getting rid of their debts, selling off the rental properties. Now that the mortgage on the Seaton Carew houses was paid off, there was no pressure on her to move out, but she always indicated she'd put them on the market at some time in the near future. After all, what use were they to one woman living on her own? Pressed on her future plans, she remained vague, however.

'I might stay in the area – it'd be a wrench to give up my job,' she'd muse.

Then in the next breath she would take quite a different tack: 'Maybe I'll move away altogether. Perhaps try living abroad...'

In his bedsit next door John would listen to the voices of his sons – still so hard to accept these deep man's voices belonged to his boys – and try to hear what they were saying. Starved of social interaction, he longed to burst through the hidden passageway and appear in front of them, seeing their expressions of shock turn to delight, giving each one of them an awkward hug. But, ever the self-disciplinarian, he'd nip those fancies in the bud as soon as they flitted into his mind, forcing himself to think instead of the new life that he and Anne would lead once this was all over. Maybe then, when they were set up somewhere in Australia or

Canada and all the fuss had died down, he might be reunited with his sons. Once the boys could see how content they were, how settled, they'd understand why they'd done what they had. He was sure of it.

He just had to be patient.

But, as the weeks and months wore on with agonising slowness, it became obvious things were going to take longer than John had hoped. Under his guidance Anne had put all the rental properties they owned around Durham on the market. But these were, as his aunt had rightly surmised, worth very little. And they'd hardly sell overnight either, so that was a long-term strategy.

Being mortgage-free on their main houses was a real relief, although he was incensed by the decision of the insurance company to halve the £50,000 payout he was hoping to get from the serious accident cover he'd taken out just months before his disappearance, on account of the body never having been found.

'It's outrageous,' he fumed when the announcement was made, seemingly unaware of the irony of a man pretending to be dead getting hot under the collar about an insurance company that wouldn't pay out in full without irrefutable proof that he was so.

Obviously they'd have to wait until all the rental properties were sold and then put the two Seaton Carew houses on the market, but they had to tread cautiously so as not to attract any suspicion. After all, Anne was a doctor's receptionist who led a very quiet life. She couldn't up sticks and move to the other side of the world all alone at the drop of a hat without raising some serious eyebrows. No, they'd have to play it very carefully.

John Darwin, expert game player, was masterminding his own

death with the same level of strategic planning as if he was executing a raid in EverQuest. It was, he firmly believed, all a question of tactics.

But even master tacticians can find that being cooped up inside 24/7 can do funny things to a person's brain, even with the run of seven bedrooms plus assorted other living spaces. Some days John Darwin felt he might spontaneously combust with boredom, thereby solving the 'acting dead' problem once and for all.

And the pressure was inevitably taking its toll on his marriage. Even the closest of couples would find it hard to survive that level of enforced togetherness, and John and Anne were feeling the strain. This was a couple who, don't forget, had spent a few weeks completely apart but were now thrown together practically every waking moment, without even the option of going for a walk to break the monotony.

It was *quantity* time, rather than quality.

John needed to get out of the house more. To this end he had to bring his alter ego 'John Jones' more to the fore. With a few small variations here and there he'd kept on with the disguise Anne so disliked, feeling his way into the character he'd invented. Armed with John Jones's date of birth and his library card, he managed to get hold of a duplicate birth certificate in this new name. Suddenly John Jones was starting to become real. So real in fact that, in the autumn of 2003, he decided to take a quite staggering risk. He would apply for a passport, using this false name but his own address and a photo of him in full Grizzly Adams-style disguise as John Jones. The local librarian, who knew him by the name on his card, John Jones, would vouch for him and sign the back of his photo. He was sure that he could get away with it.

'It's too big a risk,' Anne told him when she heard of his grand plan. 'What if they send somebody round to check?' Naturally conservative, she had visions of faceless officials descending on the house, demanding to know who this John Jones was and what he was doing there.

But the risk appealed to John's arrogant nature. He'd outwitted the authorities so far, why shouldn't his luck hold out? Besides, his frustrated wanderlust and thirst for freedom easily outweighed his desire for caution and he insisted it was a chance worth taking.

For weeks after the application was posted the Darwins lived in a state of near-constant fear, jumping each time the door of No. 4 slammed shut next door, convinced it was the police, come to expose John once and for all.

Then one morning at the door there was a package to be signed for. John could hardly believe it when he saw the name typed on the envelope: John Jones.

Anne gazed at him as he sat turning the small, maroon-coloured booklet in his hands over and over in disbelief, his fingers tracing the gold-embossed coat-of-arms on the cover. Surely it couldn't be that simple?

But it was. After months of being virtually housebound, months of staring out of windows at the same expanse of sea, he was now free to leave the country. Perhaps even more momentous was the fact that, for the first time in two years, he felt once more as if he existed in the world. At last he was a person again, with proof of his right to be among other people.

Up The Creek Without a Paddle

Over the past two years there had been few occasions to celebrate in the Darwin household, but that day in October 2003, when John Darwin officially became John Jones, was one of them.

For John the passport represented his key to a different world. It was the first sign that at last the plans he'd made were starting to fall into place. The new life overseas, the sun-drenched balcony and the early morning paddle over crystal clear waters... It was all starting to seem possible.

'This is it,' he told his wife, his eyes unnaturally bright above his ZZ Top beard. 'We're on our way.'

But with the passport came new worries for Anne Darwin. At least when he was imprisoned in the house John had been safe from prying eyes and suspicious glances. Now he was free to roam, the risks of discovery were higher than ever.

She tried to be happy, but suddenly everything seemed to be happening far too quickly. Sure, John had always talked about eventually moving abroad, but part of her had thought this would never happen. To be honest, there was a big part of her that secretly wondered whether they might just go on ad infinitum, co-existing for ever in a half-life, operating outside normal human dimensions, like Nicole Kidman in *The Others*. And while she'd found the prospect scarily oppressive just a short while ago, now she looked back on it as reassuring, almost comforting.

Meanwhile the rows between the couple escalated.

'How's it going to feel walking through Customs with you with a fake passport?' she wanted to know. 'I'll be terrified the whole time, wondering whether this is the time something comes up on that computer system of theirs. I'm not a criminal, John, and neither are you. We're an ordinary couple. How did we end up here?'

But John, who'd never wanted to be 'ordinary', was buoyed up by his passport success. Wasn't this proof enough that you can beat the system if you're just clever enough and prepared to take a few risks, he argued. Wasn't history made by people prepared to think outside of the box, as they said in the States? Being a criminal these days didn't carry the stigma it had done years ago. Many of the smartest people in the world were prepared to stretch a few laws to breaking point. She just had to stop thinking like a convent schoolgirl, governed by rules and regulations.

The more he thought about it the more he liked the idea of being able to slip in and out of different countries, right under the noses of the so-called authorities, flying off to foreign parts in search of the ultimate dream destination.

It was almost like playing EverQuest. Except this time, it felt like it was for real.

5
INTERNATIONAL MAN
OF MYSTERY

The new passport ushered in a new era at No. 3. Now John had a new name and a new identity he decided that it was time to make up for all those lost months cooped up at home. For him it wasn't just a few pages of stapled-together bureaucracy, but literally a passport to a new life.

And boy, did he need one.

However he might have envisaged his period of incarceration in the bosom of the family home, it wasn't how it had turned out. Far from being united in their predicament, the stress of fugitive life was forcing him and his wife increasingly apart.

John resented the fact that she was free to come and go as she pleased, while he was still virtually tied to the house, but even more than that he resented the fact that, as sole living partner in their relationship, she was in control of all the money. To be brutally honest, this was something he hadn't really thought about before he did his vanishing act. After all, he and Anne had been together 29 years, so surely it didn't matter whose name was on the chequebooks and credit cards, did it? But by this time their relationship was on far rockier ground. Where once they'd been a united couple, now they were very definitely two individuals, with very different ideas.

As sole owner of the bank account Anne liked the feeling that it was she who controlled the purse strings for a change. The only one now earning a salary, she enjoyed feeling that she was financially in charge for once and she wasn't about to give up her newly won independence without a struggle. But for John, obsessed since childhood with money – the making, saving and spending of it – realising that he had no bank account and no credit was a huge blow and increased the resentment between them.

Anne's gripes were still centred round her insistence that John had done this to them, that he had got them into their current situation without consulting her.

'I never would have gone along with it,' she'd sob many a time.

And yet one could be forgiven for thinking, as John often did, that the lady doth protest too much. Of course she had known his intentions, she'd understood exactly what he was planning, and why. And so it seemed impossible to understand how, when he disappeared, she'd acted so surprised.

At cross purposes much of the time, and living under the constant threat of discovery, the couple found their arguments increasing in frequency and intensity. Many times Anne, who possessed a stubborn, iron streak despite her librarian-like appearance, would storm out of the house, slamming the front door behind her, enjoying as she did so the knowledge that John didn't have the same luxury but was forced to remain indoors, simmering like rice in a pressure cooker, waiting until dark to slip out the back door.

Getting into the car, she'd drive blindly away from Seaton Carew, muttering angrily under her breath, her knuckles tight on the steering wheel.

I could just keep on driving, she'd think to herself. I could disappear just like he did. See how he likes that!

Or, whenever she was particularly upset, she'd imagine driving to a police station to turn John in. 'It's about my husband,' she might say to the officer on duty. 'He's not really dead, he's back home, having a cup of tea.'

For a few blissful moments she'd allow herself to imagine the sheer relief of having confessed, of no longer being forced to carry this leaden secret around inside her like a tumour. Inevitably, sooner or later, the inescapable reality of her situation would hit her all over again and she'd have to pull over to the side of the road before tears blurred her vision.

She was implicated in this whole ridiculous mess, so she couldn't give John up without also admitting her own involvement. They'd both be in it up to their necks. Besides, how could she tell her sons that she'd turned their father in to the police? After everything he'd done, they'd both done, to claw their way out of debt, how could she explain having willingly plunged them back into an even greater financial nightmare?

With her head bent over the steering wheel so as to shield her face from passing motorists (even in the midst of her despair she worried about making a scene), she would let the hot tears come, her breath escaping in half-swallowed sobs that shook her neat, orderly frame.

One terrible time she ran out the house and across the road to the very stretch of beach from where John had gone missing. Sitting on a bench, gazing out to sea, she imagined wading out there and losing herself in the vast bleakness of the ocean, giving in to the misery that never seemed to be so very far away. But then she thought again of her loving sons, who'd already gone through the agony of losing one parent. She knew she couldn't do that to them. However she looked at it, there was no way out. Whether they liked or loathed each other, she and John were now shackled in this miserable charade – for better, for worse.

With relations with Anne at an all-time low, John increasingly turned to the computer for escape. Through playing EverQuest he had amassed a network of new cyber friends, scattered throughout the world. These were relationships that could spring up quickly and, in some cases, might intensify with alarming speed.

When you meet someone in real life you're immediately held back by the need to process the signs they give off with their looks, body language, dress sense and general demeanour. This creates an instant barrier to intimacy, requiring a big investment of time and determination to break through and build upon. But now the Internet removes all such obstacles. The person on the screen arrives unfettered by prejudgements or expectations; there's no context – kids, clothes, environment – to colour your opinion or dictate what can or can't be broached. With the Internet you can be who you want to be, discuss what you want to. And there are no barriers – not even being, well, dead.

And so Darwin the Druid, who'd worked for years in the same prison without making any close friends, was able to form Internet attachments – many of them with women – in a way that he'd never managed in real life. Free from the awkwardness he often felt when socialising with people he didn't know, John was able to be at once debonair, mysterious, wise and flirtatious. To the women with whom he was in contact in America and Canada he wasn't a non-man, confined to a bedsit unless his wife allowed him out through a cupboard, but a witty, sophisticated, urbane British adventurer who talked knowledgeably about property and shares, and boasted a love of the outdoors. In effect, having died, he was now 'rebirthing' himself in a mould far more in keeping with his own inflated self-image than the previous, socially inept incarnation.

He struck up a cyber relationship with a 41-year-old mother-of-three that he met through EverQuest. Kelly Steele, aka Guurg (a male frog), lived in a suburb of Kansas City on the Kansas/Missouri border and had been playing the online game with her family for years. Recently they'd reached a critical point where they were in dire need of extra points, but for that they required the services of a Druid. Luckily for her there was one online at the time – the romantically named Cedum – who accepted her invitation to play with them. Perhaps unluckily for her, though, Cedum the Saviour was none other than John Darwin.

At first she was delighted with her new playing partner. Not only was Cedum available, he was also good. For hours each day the two played in partnership, helping each other out, while chatting about this and that. Kelly told Cedum that her husband Jamie was away for long stretches at a time, working with a team to build specialist fences, and with her kids at school she was left with a lot of time on her hands during the day. For his part Cedum confided that he was a widower called John Jones, whose wife had died of cancer and that he was desperately lonely.

'I feel sorry for the guy,' Kelly told her family. 'He's just after some company.'

But the more time they spent online together the more John opened up to this stranger halfway across the world.

'I used to work for the prison office,' he told her, clearly hoping to impress. 'But I made enough from my rental properties that I could afford to retire.' Just in case Kelly thought that made him sound a bit staid and elderly, Darwin was quick to tell her of his passion for kayaking and other virile outdoor pursuits.

Early on, Kelly probably realised that Cedum was flirting with her, but she laughed it off. After all, he lived far enough away that she could be sure he wasn't about to leap on her, and anyway the guy was obviously harmless. And so she kept up her online gaming sessions with him and tried to brush off his increasingly flirtatious messages, even when he got hold of some headphones and started talking to her in his real human voice, rather than just with words typed on a screen.

Over the course of their cyber 'friendship' Kelly told John all about the outskirts of Kansas City, where she lived.

'If you're into renting out property, you should take a look round here,' she joked. 'It's so cheap you could practically buy a house on your credit card.'

As John seemed genuinely interested she elaborated, telling him about the ghost towns around Kansas City, farming areas where nothing ever happened and property carried bargain-basement price tags. To her surprise John Jones, UK-based retired prison officer and amateur kayaker, seemed to find the idea of a farm in America's remote heartland rather thrilling.

'How much would it cost?' he asked. 'What kind of place would you get? How close would your nearest neighbours be?'

If Kelly thought he'd be put off when she told him that some places were so isolated you'd be lucky to see anyone from one week to the next, she was wrong. He seemed enchanted by the idea. 'That would suit me down to the ground,' he enthused. 'Somewhere quiet, with a small population.'

It sounded like some kind of a joke and Kelly imagined John would forget about the idea by the next day or the next week, but over the days that followed he kept returning to the subject, seemingly won over by the notion of investing in the Midwestern prairie. 'Is a foreigner entitled to buy land?' he wanted to know. 'What kind of money can you make by doing a place up and selling it on?'

She grew increasingly confused. One minute John seemed to be talking about moving over there himself, the next he'd be asking about the rental market as if thinking about becoming an absentee landlord. Then, when she mentioned the possibility of doing up a place to run as a cattle ranch, she got the distinct impression he was imagining himself in the saddle, patrolling his property on horseback. Middle England meets Brokeback Mountain.

Up The Creek Without a Paddle

If her new cyber pal had been there in the flesh his body language and expressions might have given her more clues as to what was really going on in his mind, but in the absence of a face-to-face meeting she found it hard to get a handle on what he was after. But gradually one thing became increasingly obvious: John the Druid was deadly serious.

So what was going through his mind? Was he really imagining a life for himself in the wilderness of the Midwest, doing something rugged and outdoorsy, somewhere off the beaten track where nobody knew who he was? Or was he, as Kelly first surmised, interested only in the potential profit from buying and selling on?

Quite possibly even John didn't know the answer to that. In his self-imposed solitary confinement, increasingly cold-shouldered by his resentful 'widow', his thoughts were becoming ever more confused. The former science and maths teacher had always prided himself on his clear linear thought processes, but now he often found himself going round in circles, searching for a way out of his predicament, but more frustratingly ending up right back where he started.

Whatever the motivation, Kansas became almost an obsession. It seemed to tick all his boxes. It was remote, it was cheap, there were no nosy neighbours watching your every movement. He could use it as a bolthole, or mastermind the whole operation from afar. And there was his new best friend Kelly to add a little flirtatious frisson to the whole deal.

Not to put too fine a point on it, relations with Anne were not what either of them would have wished for. Far from being the warm, cosy love-nest he'd fondly imagined during his weeks of self-imposed exile following his disappearance, No. 3 felt more like Cold Comfort Farm. In fact there were times when John received the distinct impression that his wife of 30 years actively wished him dead. Again.

When she came through the door at the end of a day's work she could hardly bear to look at him, and as for physical intimacy, well, that was becoming as much of a distant memory as his former self. Everything he said seemed to irritate his wife, who seemed to be perpetually simmering with a just-disguised anger that was looking for any excuse to erupt to the surface.

Stung by what he considered to be her ingratitude and lack of empathy, John spent more and more time holed up in his bedsit, relying on his cyber chums for company, particularly Kelly. Sometimes he'd sit so long at his computer talking to her that when he stood up his legs felt weak with disuse.

He knew she was married, but it was clear that her husband spent long periods away, which must mean, he convinced himself, that she was in need of someone to lavish time and attention upon her. Both of which he had in spades. He was quite proud of the image of himself that he felt he'd managed to convey – a man of the world who'd made a few astute investments and was looking to diversify; a keen sportsman with a tragic past.

The more time he spent talking to Kelly the more convinced he became that she understood him in a way that Anne, increasingly, seemed not to. The area around Kansas City, he was sure, was the answer to his immediate problems. He was seduced by the idea of its wide open spaces, where a man who wanted to be lost could become so, without having to shut himself away like a rat in a hole.

Still portraying himself as a wealthy widower, he asked Kelly to research likely properties. They'd be in a kind of partnership, he told her, just as they were online. She'd find the place, and as he wasn't a US citizen she'd also buy it in her name and do it up, maybe even run it as a working farm, and he'd provide the funding. Then they'd split the profits, with Kelly repaying her share of the initial investment. For the suburban housewife from a town where so little happens that the erection of a new phone box is front-page news, this all sounded too good to be true.

And there were plenty of people who warned her that it probably was too good to be true. Men from thousands of miles away just didn't hand over money to people they met on the Internet, at least not without expecting something pretty major in return.

Kelly's husband Jamie was particularly suspicious. Just what was this John Jones's angle, anyway? But she insisted he was on the level – just a man with spare cash who wanted to do something a bit different and who recognised a good business opportunity. She decided to take him at his word and start scouting around for properties – after all, what did she have to lose?

It wasn't long before she found the perfect place – a derelict ten-acre farm in Kincaid, south of Kansas City, on the market for just £14,000. It would need lots of work, she told John, but it had great potential. At this stage she still half-expected him to back down and was prepared to feel totally outraged if it turned out he'd been leading her on all this time. So, imagine her surprise when, unbelievably, the money for the purchase plus renovations appeared in her bank account – wired from a UK account.

Now she was able to silence the doubters who'd chided her for being so gullible. She'd been right to trust her instincts. John Jones was a nice man with too much time on his hands and more money than sense. This could be a real turning point for her, she felt; a once-in-a-lifetime opportunity had just fallen into her lap.

She went ahead with the purchase of the farm and started the considerable task of restoring the disused, weather-beaten farmhouse to a habitable state. 'Sometimes,' she told people, 'chances come along when you're least expecting them, and it's up to you to grab hold of them.'

Now everyone knows that dead men don't cash cheques, so quite where John Darwin, deceased, managed to get hold of that amount of money is something of a mystery. He had access to his wife's banking passwords and pin numbers so it's just conceivable that he could have shifted large amounts of cash around without her knowledge, or perhaps he had convinced her that it was for something else.

By this stage Anne was already deeply suspicious of all the time John was spending on the computer. Once she'd even overheard him talking to a woman on the headset he had attached to his keyboard. She knew it was a woman from the tone of voice he was using – low and shockingly intimate, punctuated with nervous laughter. She'd felt angry and humiliated – here she was, carrying all this weight around on her shoulders, while he was blithely chatting up strangers from the Internet. And despite the sorry state of their relationship, she was also scared. She wasn't an independent-spirited pioneering type – she was a wife of 30 years who didn't know anything other than being a wife. If John left her who would she be?

'Go on then, find someone else, I don't care!' she'd retorted when they argued about it later. 'She's welcome to you! Let her cope with having a dead man hanging round the house all the time.'

In this spirit of wilful indifference, she deliberately refused to ask him about his plans, even when he began to show signs of preparing for a trip. It was, after all, his life, she reflected – in a manner of speaking.

Kelly Steele had been busy convincing herself that her dealings with the mysterious Mr Jones were entirely professional. Even so, when, in May 2004, he announced that he was coming over to Kansas City to inspect his new investment for himself, she felt a twinge of anxiety. After all, she really didn't know anything about the guy. He could turn out to be a total flake. And he seemed so anxious to stay with her family rather than in a hotel, which also set her on edge. Having a business relationship with someone you met on the Net was one thing, letting them into your home was quite another.

As the day drew nearer to his arrival her nervousness just increased. She cursed herself for having agreed to him staying with her. She had a nine-year-old daughter living with her. What could she have been thinking? To quell her rising panic she kept reminding herself that she'd liked him when they first started chatting online. He was just a lonely man, looking for excitement, she told herself. It wasn't as though she didn't know him – they'd been 'talking' for weeks. Everything would be fine.

International Man of Mystery

Waiting in the Arrivals hall at the airport, she felt a deep sense of foreboding settle over her. Don't be silly, she scolded herself, you're just creating problems for yourself that don't even exist.

When the passengers from John's plane began to stream out through Customs she strained for a first glimpse of the man she'd been cyber-befriending for weeks. For a while she didn't spot him – after all, she had only a somewhat grainy photo for identification – but then her eyes kept coming back to rest on one lone figure who stood, also scanning the crowd, as if looking for someone. Already thudding wildly, her heart seemed to seize up inside her. Surely this couldn't be...? Surely he wasn't...?

But it could... And he was.

Luckily for Kelly, John had got rid of the unkempt beard for his big trip. But, obviously feeling the need to retain a certain amount of facial furniture so as to match the photo in his new passport, he'd cultivated a pair of bushy sideburns and Denis Healy-style eyebrows. Along with his balding pate and narrow, sunken eyes, this was not, it has to be said, a particularly good look.

As they made their introductions Kelly's discomfort grew. The man didn't once look her in the eyes. Instead his gaze seemed to glide right off her and he'd stare off to one side while talking, as if in a kind of trance. All through the drive back to her house she fretted. She knew right away that she didn't want this stranger staying in her house, but how was she going to get out of it?

But while she was agonising, John Darwin, though one wouldn't have guessed it from the outside, was jubilant. Ever since he booked his flight he'd been terrified about the prospect of using his new passport. What if there was some irregularity?

What if the authorities decided to make more thorough checks on Mr John Jones?

Standing in the queue waiting to hand it over, he'd felt almost sick with nerves. What if everything was to come crashing down now, after all he'd been through? Had he been insane to take this sort of risk? Even when the official handed him back his passport with scarcely a second glance, he hardly dared to relax. He'd still have to repeat the procedure at the other end and everyone knew how stringent the American airport officials were after 9/11.

So, by the time he emerged unchallenged into the Arrivals lounge at Kansas City International Airport, he was quite light-headed with relief. And there was Kelly to meet him, just as she'd promised. Although he didn't really take a proper look at her, he liked what he'd seen so far – curvy, with long, straight, brown hair and wide-set, pale-blue eyes, she was completely different to Anne in every respect, which, given the current strained state of affairs between husband and wife, pleased him immensely.

OK, so the initial meeting at the airport was a little stilted, but he wasn't the kind of person who was at ease in new situations, so he wasn't overly concerned. No, things were turning out exactly as he'd hoped.

Ruskin Heights, to the south of Kansas City, is a 1950s-built community, still famous mostly for the tornado that hit the area in 1957, causing massive damage. It was there, to her modest house, that Kelly reluctantly brought John Darwin after her trip to the airport.

During the journey nothing had happened to quell her fears about the strange man that she'd so blithely gone into business

88

with, and as he carried his bags through the front door already she was starting to wish she'd never invited him to stay. Whatever did or didn't happen during John's stay remains somewhat hazy. Anne Darwin would later tell a courtroom that he'd had an affair while he was in America – an assertion Kelly Steele would adamantly refute. Whatever the truth, despite the 'special relationship' John clearly believed the two of them had, it wasn't long before he moved out of Kelly's house and into a nearby motel. And if he was hoping this might get things back on course after the rocky start he was sorely mistaken.

John Jones was a man looking for affection. He'd cut himself off from everyone he knew and his wife was constantly angry with him. He'd half-hoped that meeting up with Kelly would fill the empty space in his life and his heart, so when it became clear that she now wanted theirs to be a purely business relationship he felt disappointed and not a little put out. He was sure he hadn't imagined the spark between them.

'Surely you must know some single women out here who'd be looking for someone like me?' he asked her hopefully.

But she just shook her head, entirely unable to think of any circumstances where anyone might be looking for someone like him.

John grew steadily more disillusioned with the whole Kansas City plan, but the farm was OK – a dilapidated, white clapboard structure surrounded by countryside. The first time he visited, pushing open the rickety front door and peering in through the shuttered-up gloom, he'd been quite excited. Despite the absence of electricity, water or even floorboards, he'd imagined moving straight in, tearing up his return plane ticket and throwing himself into rural life, with Kelly as his guide. But, as the relationship deteriorated, so too did his dreams of a new life in the American wilderness. Far from being the soul mate he'd fondly been imagining, she became more distant the longer he knew her. If he tried to suggest going anywhere that wasn't to do with business she made excuses or changed the subject. He'd hoped to impress her with his worldliness, but it became clear that the only world she was interested in was one without her cyber-partner in it. In addition to the initial £14,000 investment he'd also spent a further £15,000 on doing the place up, but as far as he could see he had absolutely nothing to show for it.

By the time he was due to leave he had come to the painful conclusion that Kansas City was not the brave new world he'd been hoping for. He'd thrown his soul and his money into what he hoped would be a new chapter in his life only to find that it had turned out to be a dead end. As he sat on the plane, preparing to return to the life he'd come to loathe, his thoughts were dark and brooding. After all the sacrifices he'd made to get that money, to have tossed it all away on a bad hunch seemed cruel beyond belief.

Kelly hadn't proved an ideal partner for him in either a business or a romantic sense, and he was completely devastated that all his dreams, not to mention his sizeable financial outlay, had come to nothing. Always a proud man, he was going home, tail between his legs, to who knew what kind of reception from his wife, all a far cry from the triumphant life-change he'd been hoping for.

For her part Kelly was delighted to see him leave. With John out of the way she was free to focus on the investment she'd made with his money. She began renovating the little farm with a view to perhaps turning it into a cattle ranch, as they had discussed. But her relief was to be short-lived. John hadn't been gone long before he started sending her messages in a very different tone from the playful, bantering ones he'd sent as Cedum. He demanded that she should get a move on with the renovations so that the house was ready to sell on again. Every few days he'd send another message, asking for a progress report. The tone became increasingly intimidating, the language ever more threatening.

Increasingly alarmed, Kelly was soon to regret that she'd ever asked for cyber help from Cedrum the Druid, or his alter ego John Jones.

There are some relationships that really ought to remain virtual – and this was clearly one of them.

6
ITCHY FEET

For a while the disappointing American trip dampened John's enthusiasm for foreign travel. But as 2004 drew to a close, bringing with it a cold fug that seemed to hang heavily in the air like a damp cloth and caused the windows of No. 3 to run with condensation and faint clouds of mist to form each time anybody spoke, once again he started to fantasise about moving overseas.

It would be the answer to everything, he decided. Away from the constant stress of life in Seaton Carew, he and Anne would kick-start their flagging relationship and begin all over again, putting their money into a development or a project that would give them an occupation as well as an income. He began reading up about Australia, Canada and Cyprus. It was the last that he returned to again and again. Cyprus had everything he was looking for – a mild climate, plenty of opportunities for outdoor sports, plus it was near enough to the UK to allow Anne to pop back and forth to see the boys. And the fact that it offered a preferential tax rate on pensions and zero inheritance tax obviously didn't hurt either.

'Let's go take a look,' he proposed, suddenly unable to bear the idea of yet another afternoon where darkness had already settled in by 3.30 in the afternoon. 'It'll be a holiday for us. God knows, we deserve it.'

But Anne was torn. She was still seething about John's American trip. Not that she knew many details, but she was sure he'd gone out to meet a woman. The atmosphere between them had been tenser than ever since his return. Plus, she didn't know how she could bear the anxiety of knowing she'd be travelling with someone who was not only officially dead but also travelling on a fraudulent passport. She had never been in trouble with the authorities, even at school, and the thought of being challenged by Customs officials in full view of other travellers made her feel quite sick.

At the same time she was desperate for a holiday. The past year had been so unimaginably stressful. If they were away, somewhere no one knew them, they'd be able to be a normal couple again, to do things other husbands and wives take for granted, like walking down the road side by side, or having a meal out. They might even start to rediscover some common ground again, free of the pressures that made them always so short with each other.

In the end the idea of going out in public without the constant fear that someone was going to spot them, without checking every passing door, every shop window, proved irresistibly seductive and she stonily agreed to a week's holiday. The tickets were booked for November 2004.

Itchy Feet

For both of them the days leading up to the flight were even more tense than normal. John tried to quieten his nerves by thinking through everything that needed to be done, making lists, looking things up on the Internet. He wanted to make the most of their time in Cyprus by looking at different properties to buy and talking to developers about maybe having a house specially built. John, with his need for control, had always dreamed of designing his own home, built to just his specifications. Perhaps this might be their chance.

Anne's imagination was less easy to rein in. At nights she dreamed about walking along airport corridors, her heart thumping in her chest, just as in *Midnight Express*, where the film's hero is caught trying to smuggle drugs on board a plane in Turkey. The fact that John had already travelled once on his new passport did little to calm her nerves. Again and again she'd picture the scene where he would hand his passport over to officials and they'd glance down at their computers, then up at him, then back again, beckoning over reinforcements – 'If you wouldn't mind stepping this way, sir? Madam?'

She imagined the terror of it, and the shame and the humiliation. Being pulled aside in front of all those people: 'There appears to be a problem, sir.'

She'd always led such a blameless, squeaky-clean life and now, at the age of 52, when most people had put their wild pasts well behind them, she had turned herself into an outlaw. It was funny how, all her life, she had been comforted by the sight of a policeman in uniform, secure in the knowledge that he was there to protect her interests. And now just a glimpse of a blue light on a car or the top of a policeman's hat was enough to send her into a cold sweat. At an age when most career criminals are considering hanging up their balaclavas and running a nice B&B on the Costa del Sol, she had become someone who existed outside the law.

The night before they were due to fly she was so nervous she hardly slept, going over and over in her head the different scenarios that could await them. And yet the journey went off without a hitch. John had toned down his wild facial hair disguise, while Anne, who had the natural look of a born Sunday school teacher, didn't draw a second glance. They breezed through passport control, her heart thudding like a pogo stick in her ribcage. The other passengers, their bright holiday T-shirts concealed under macs and quilted jackets, were far too excited about their forthcoming holidays to pay any attention to the drab, middle-aged couple in their midst.

As the plane taxied down the runway, preparing to take off, she finally allowed herself to relax, feeling suddenly as if a great weight she hadn't even known she was carrying was being lifted from her, in the same way the plane was lifting from the ground.

They were free.

The Darwins hadn't been in Cyprus long before it became clear that being dead hadn't taught John Darwin any humility.

A patient estate agent showed them plenty of properties, but none was quite right for the demanding couple.

'We're much better off getting our own place built,' said John irritably, after yet another property had been found wanting.

Anne liked the idea of having a house custom-made — a

completely new home for a completely new start. It had a certain symbolism, plus, of course, she'd get to choose all the fixtures and fittings, or more likely John would probably pick them and she'd go along with it. It would be such a pleasant change from the oppressive, faded period gloom of their Seaton Carew house.

The couple was introduced to a local architect who would be able to draw up plans for them and for a brief time it seemed as if this would be the escape they'd been dreaming of. And yet, almost from the start, the cracks were beginning to show in the façade of their Cyprus dream home.

'Everything is so inefficient here,' was John's favourite refrain from the moment they landed. The airport was chaotic, the transport links difficult. And once they started looking into buying land and constructing their own property, the potential problems multiplied. There was so much red tape involved with everything, so much paperwork. The architect promised to draw up plans, but nothing materialised.

Anne watched the blissful week of relaxation she'd planned disappear into thin air like heat haze off a tarmac road. There were too many appointments to be kept, too many hissed quarrels in the back of estate agents' cars. It wasn't so much that she and John weren't getting on, just that there were so many complications to everything they tried to do.

By the time they got on the plane to return home, already they were having misgivings – not helped by the nerve-racking wait at passport control.

All through the journey home they talked over living in Cyprus. On the one hand it was so convenient, with so many budget flights from the UK every day, but on the other hand, wouldn't the slowness of it all drive them crazy? Driving back to Seaton Carew through the November gloom, both were tempted to think that anything, surely, must be better than this — a return to house arrest for John, and to life on eggshells for Anne. But when days and weeks passed without word from the architect they grew increasingly disillusioned. For so long John had dreamed of a foreign paradise where they could indulge in an outdoor life away from the rat race back home, but the more he thought about it the less Cyprus seemed to fit the bill.

'I know what you mean,' Anne agreed. 'It didn't feel exactly, well, us. Did it?' They decided to abandon their plans of moving there and turn their attentions to somewhere else.

The week in Cyprus had proved, if nothing else, that they were able to travel without coming under suspicion. What it hadn't done, however, was breathe new life into their tired relationship. Settling back into No. 3 was like returning to a prison cell after a brief spell on parole (something John, with his long career in the prison service, knew all about). After the clear skies of Cyprus, the overcast gloom of Seaton Carew in winter was hard to accept. All around them people were preparing for Christmas with that low-level buzz of anticipation that somehow gets you through the bleak, early December days. But for Anne and John the festive plans were muted, to say the least. She was hoping to see the boys over Christmas, but naturally, seeing the boys meant not seeing John.

While his wife went about the preamble to Christmas, buying presents, writing cards, attending little Christmas drinks at work, John would sit sulking at his computer, dashing off increasingly curt messages to Kelly and brooding on the impossible narrowness of his life.

Nor did the New Year bring much to celebrate. Anne was trying to be more patient with John – after all, he had so little in his life now and without her he had absolutely nothing. But despite her good intentions, she would still end up snapping at him when he stuck a little too closely to her at the end of a busy day when she just wanted to unwind. The arguments followed a depressingly predictable path, always ending up, no matter what the original cause, in accusations and recriminations.

How could you have…? What gave you the right to…?

If John Darwin had been hard to live with when he was alive, Anne would reflect as the slam of the interconnecting door resounded in her ears, now he was dead he was well-nigh impossible.

Meanwhile, alone in his little bolthole-cum-prison, he would pour out his frustrations through the computer. Kelly, in particular, became a target for his pent-up rage. The Kansas City woman had, he now decided, led him on. She'd made him believe there could be something between them and then been so cold to him once he'd travelled out to see her. She'd also led him to believe there was a quick profit to be made from property in her neck of the woods and this, it was becoming increasingly clear, was far from the case. He'd been a fool to part with that money and now he wanted it back – or at least her share of the costs.

Back in Ruskin Heights, Kelly grew ever more wary with each message that arrived in her inbox from johnjones1850@yahoo.com. At first the tone was just clipped, but then it started to take on a more sinister note as Darwin realised the renovation project would take far longer than he'd anticipated.

Finally, in March 2005, came an email that left her terrified and trembling. According to Kelly, John, who'd at first seemed so mild-mannered and pathetic with his sad story of his dead wife, warned her that he had employed a New York debt collection agency to reclaim the money she owed him. The company had photos of her and her family (her daughter and sister were particularly singled out), he told her, the implication being that something terrible might happen to those closest to her if she didn't pay up. He urged her to check the brakes on her car and hinted at that famous scene in *The Godfather* where Don Corleone wakes up to find the head of his favourite horse on the pillow next to him.

'Things will happen and continue to happen unless you repay all of my money,' he allegedly wrote. 'Let the nightmare begin.'

Not surprisingly, Kelly Steele was frightened beyond any fear she'd ever experienced in her life. She had naively, some would say foolishly, entered into a business relationship with a man she barely knew and now she was paying the heaviest of prices.

'Don't *ever* go out without telling me exactly where you are,' she told her daughter, nearly hysterical with fear and worry.

The night after receiving the email she went to sleep with a shotgun by her side and a knife under her pillow, wishing more than anything that John Jones had remained a fantasy figure from an online game, someone she could switch off with the click of a mouse. If a thing seemed too good to be true, she'd learned to her cost, it probably was.

Itchy Feet

With his Kansas City dreams now gone up in smoke, John Darwin was once again restless and bored, pacing the perimeters of the house as if trying to expand its walls by sheer force of will.

'Can't you just relax?' Anne would snap, irritated by his twitchy energy, longing to be left in peace. Given the tensions between them, she was relieved when John started taking off for short periods. Though he couldn't do any bank transactions, he had access to her passwords and pin numbers, so getting hold of cash was no longer a problem. Sometimes he'd tell her where he was going, other times she'd get home from work and know immediately, from the lightness of atmosphere in the house, that he was gone.

Then it was as though everything in her – every muscle, every nerve ending – unclenched and unfurled, likely when you sink into a hot bath at the end of a tense day. Without his hovering, brooding presence she could throw the curtains wide and let the light infiltrate all the dark, shrinking corners of the house, unafraid of detection or remonstration.

So where did John Darwin, recently deceased, go on his jaunts away from Seaton Carew? Well, for a start – and it was a very big start – he travelled right away from the stultifying atmosphere at No. 3. Oppressed by the 24-hour confinement of his multi-bedroom prison, every step away from The Cliff felt like a Neil Armstrong-style stride towards freedom.

The facial hair and woolly hat he often wore gave him an illusion of safety behind which he could regard a world that seemed at times to be moving on without him. And the passport in his pocket was a solid, tangible licence to be at large. Whenever he was nervous, just feeling the smooth weightiness of it was enough to reassure him that it would be OK, that he had the right to be out walking in the world.

Sometimes he just got on a train and went off to explore places he'd never visited before. There was always a thrill as familiar scenery dissolved into unknown rolling countryside which gave way to urban sprawl, and then to glimpses of rugged coastline. He'd always go for places where he could make the most of being outdoors, revelling in being able to get up every morning and be outside in the open within minutes, regardless of who he might bump into, or how crowded the area was.

He particularly loved to go fishing. There was something about being outside for hours on end, just absorbing nature in all its serene beauty, that made his unquiet soul temporarily still. And after being thrown on Anne's company for so long, he relished the silent companionship of the other fishermen. No one pestered him with questions or tried to make overloud conversation, but at the same time there was a sense of quiet camaraderie, an underlying bond of brotherhood. United by a palpable need for their own space, much as their outsized umbrellas, the anglers formed a loose collective of fiercely private individuals and that suited him down to the ground.

Sometimes on those occasions he'd go by his passport name of John Jones. Other times he'd concoct another persona, introducing himself perhaps as John Williams, a plain, unassuming 'good bloke' kind of name that no one would question or remember. Sometimes the easy fellowship that exists among anglers would instill in him such a sense of confidence and well-being that he'd let down the guard that had by now become second nature. One time he struck up a 'fishing friendship' with a dockyard worker from Cornwall called Matt Autie, while fishing on a lake near Penzance.

'I've done a Reggie Perrin,' John confided, after the two had swapped the usual pleasantries. 'I've gone missing. It worked out better for me and my wife.'

If Matt was surprised at having a relative stranger unburden himself he didn't show it. Fishing was a sport full of people looking for an escape from something: jobs they hated, fraught relationships or money problems... John Williams, as he believed Darwin to be called, was just another man with problems, looking for time out from his life. Maybe he was a fantasist, with his Reggie Perrin story, or perhaps he really had dropped out of his old life when the going got tough. And who could blame him? Didn't everyone dream of doing exactly that from time to time? Few of the anglers sitting back contentedly in their fold-up fishing chairs by the edge of the lake would have judged a man who just wanted to quietly disappear for a time.

But while he appreciated his quiet fishing trips in far-flung corners of Britain, John Darwin wanted more. He'd always been ambitious, he'd constantly dreamed of jetting round the world at the drop of a hat. And what had it all been for, this massive leap of faith he'd taken to get his family out of debt, if not to reap the rewards of financial solvency, to spread wings that had for too long been clipped? Again and again he came back to what he increasingly regarded as the only solution to his and Anne's nightmarish situation: they must join the 500 or so Britons he'd read somewhere were leaving the country each and every day to start new lives elsewhere.

They had to move abroad.

7
THE GLOBETROTTERS

You might think that after everything that had happened to him at sea, John Darwin would give the ocean a wide berth. But you'd be wrong. As 2005 limped to a close with no change in his miserable twilight existence, he started thinking that perhaps what he really needed, the thing that was going to turn his life around was … a boat.

But not just any boat. Just as he'd always driven around in flashy cars with personalised plates, he had his eye on something that was going to make him look good and restore his status in the world. It would also need to be comfortable and well enough equipped that he and Anne could take off around the world in it, dropping anchor wherever took their fancy, free as the proverbial wind. In other words, like many other middle-aged men the world over, he wanted his own yacht.

As usual, it was the Internet that he turned to first, spending hours researching just what kind of yacht they'd need, and the best places to buy one. Despite his expensive tastes, he knew they couldn't afford to splurge all the profits from his faked death on a boat when clearly they would need a guaranteed income as they got older. So he started scouring the Net for second-hand offers, which is when he got in touch with Gibraltar-based boat dealer Robert Hopkin about a 60-foot catamaran he was selling for a client.

'I'd like to come and see it,' he told Hopkin over the phone, blasé as if he bought luxury yachts all the time. 'And no, there's no problem raising the cash.'

In fact the problem lay in persuading Anne that buying a yacht was necessarily the most sensible use of their hard-won nest egg. 'We don't know the first thing about running a yacht,' she snapped at him scornfully. 'Just grow up a bit, can't you, John?'

But he wasn't to be dissuaded. In his head he now carried the very vivid image of he and Anne sipping Chardonnay on the deck of their catamaran, then dipping into some remote harbour for dinner before gliding off again across the moonlit water, leaving no trace that they were ever there. 'It's perfect, Anne. Surely you must see that? It'll give us ultimate freedom.'

For her the idea of cruising around the world on a yacht could only be pure fantasy. It was the kind of thing that Saudi princes or the stars of American mini-series did, not doctor's receptionists from Hartlepool, but he didn't let up: 'Just picture it. We won't be tied into living in any one place, but we'll be able to go exactly where we like. And if we fall in love with somewhere we can just berth up and stay a while. It's perfect.'

The Globetrotters

In vain did she point out that a couple who were having trouble staying civil in a vast, seven-bedroom house might perhaps struggle sharing a single cabin 24/7, with nothing but the endless sea to distract them. But John had thought it all through – they wouldn't be trapped on board, he assured her. On the contrary, the world would open up to them as never before; the whole ocean would be their playground.

Of course she was well aware how he got once he'd made up his mind and obviously there was something very seductive about the idea of a life spent following the sunshine with no more taxing decision to be made than which restaurant to dine in that evening. She resigned herself to letting him work this through his system – at least it would keep him occupied for a while.

She knew that he was the kind of man who always had to have a project on the go. For a brief, crazy period he'd looked into snail breeding, then he'd moved on to making garden gnomes, of all things, to sell at car-boot sales or at Durham's indoor market, along with computer games. As a teacher he'd even bring his gnomes into school and the kids would paint them and take them home as presents for their bemused parents. So now he'd moved on from gnomes to yachts. It was the same principle in the end – the need to have something to occupy his mind, a goal to work towards.

On 12 November 2005 John Darwin, aka John Jones, turned up at Newcastle International Airport for the flight to Gibraltar. Sitting in the Departures lounge, he hid his face behind a newspaper, nervous about being seen in public so close to his hometown. Throughout the flight, which stopped off at Gatwick, he kept his head averted, sending out clear 'do not disturb' signals. He relished the image of himself that he had created in his own head – an international man of substance who thought nothing of jetting off to Spain to look over a boat, the kind of man with a spare £45,000 to spend on a luxury 'toy'.

Unfortunately, this wasn't quite the impression Robert Hopkin received when he met the mysterious Mr Jones at Gibraltar's tiny airport. To him John Jones came across as something of a strange character – the type of man who doesn't quite look you in the eye when he shakes your hand. But clearly he had money to spend, and at the end of the day that's what counted.

Gibraltar airport is a one-off. More like a collection of prefab huts tacked together than an international airport, its runway passes straight across the territory's main road, causing crowds of disgruntled pedestrians to mass behind the barriers whenever a plane lands or takes off. Once free of the airport, it was another hour's drive westwards to the marina on the Costa de la Luz where the catamaran that John had already set his heart on was berthed.

Driving into the town of Puerto de Santa María, just north of Cadiz, John couldn't help feeling slightly disappointed. If he'd fondly been imagining an area dazzling with *Footballers' Wives*-style bling he was sorely mistaken, the approach being flanked by garages, industrial plants and run-down abandoned buildings. But nearing the town itself, with its cobbled streets, shady squares and historic castle, he brightened up considerably. This was more like it! It was a good way to start his new life as a global adventurer.

The marina itself seemed to sparkle as the winter sun reflected off the glittering surfaces of sea and several million pounds' worth of gleaming, state-of-the-art, white and chrome vessels. By the time Robert Hopkin showed him the catamaran that he'd travelled so far to see he was already predisposed to fall in love with it, imagining himself spending his life in places like this, dining in style at one of the marina restaurants.

The *Boonara* was an impressive-looking 1970s Solaris ketch. It had been in the same family for years, but now the owner had died his children were reluctantly selling it. It was equipped for blue-water cruising and could in effect take the Darwins all round the world. John was ecstatic.

On the drive back Robert Hopkin tried to make conversation with his clearly enraptured new client but the middle-aged man with the balding pate and slightly wild hair wouldn't be drawn. The only things the boat dealer managed to ascertain were that John Jones was retired, that he planned to buy the boat with his wife and that money was no object.

After Jones had flown back to Newcastle Robert Hopkin received a few email messages from the man's wife, Anne, asking various questions about the catamaran and the sale. An experienced yacht broker, Hopkin had learned to spot when someone was really interested as opposed to window shopping, and so he wasn't too surprised when, a few days after he'd flown home, John called to say he was willing to pay the full £45,000 asking price for the *Boonara*. 'We'll transfer the deposit over right away,' he told him, affecting a casual attitude he was far from feeling.

Sure enough, £1,000 duly appeared in the brokering firm's account, transferred from an account in the name of Anne Darwin. Robert Hopkin didn't find the discrepancy in surnames odd – after all, many women kept their own names these days, and in Spain it was particularly common for a married woman to retain her father's surname. He set about drawing up a sales document in which the purchaser was listed as one John Jones, 4 The Cliff, Seaton Carew, Hartlepool, Teesside, UK, TS25 1AB.

Back in Seaton Carew, next door at No. 3 there was a palpable air of excitement as the Darwins waited for news of their latest purchase. Anne was torn between anxiety at the idea of spending so much on a boat of all things, while being swept along by John's infectious enthusiasm and thirst for adventure. But just as it seemed the deal was in the bag, things started to go sour. The family who were selling the boat announced they'd like to remove some personal items from the *Boonara*, including an old barometer which had been in place when John first viewed the boat.

Robert Hopkin didn't imagine it would be too much of a problem, but he reckoned without his mysterious client's volatile temper. If there was one thing John Darwin couldn't stand it was other people thinking they could get one over on him – ironic though that might be, coming from a man who had faked his own death to defraud the system. 'The deal's off,' he wrote in a furious email.

Not surprisingly the boat broker was exceedingly put out. He'd spent a lot of his own time on the sale and couldn't believe John Jones was now going to throw it all away in a fit of pique. Yet incredibly, that's exactly what happened. Luckily for Hopkin he managed to secure a second buyer just a few weeks later, but the Darwins were left badly burned by the episode. Not only had they lost their £1,000 deposit, but now John had apparently lost all enthusiasm for his yacht plan. If that was the kind of thing that happened in the yacht-owning community he didn't want to be part of it.

Licking his wounds and trying not to compare the dark, brooding mid-winter North Sea through his window with the sparkling Med of his dreams, he went back to the drawing board.

As if No. 3 didn't have enough room already with its seven bedrooms and grand reception rooms, it also boasted an attic at the top of the building, with a small, round window that gave a nautical-style view of the sea, and at the very bottom, below street level, a basement. Over the door to the basement hung a stuffed toy in the shape of a gargoyle, next to a printed notice, both put there as a joke by one of the Darwin sons some years before and never taken down.

'Abandon Hope All Who Enter Here' read the notice in large capital letters. At the time it was Blu-Tacked up, the sign had made John smile but when 2006 crept apologetically in, bringing with it an unpleasant reminder of how everything had changed in a year, it seemed less of a harmless joke than a dire indictment of what their lives in Seaton Carew had become. Every time he passed under it he was struck afresh by the unwitting aptness of the sentiment because by this time the prevailing mood in No. 3 was one of hopelessness and near despair. Something had to be done.

In the basement was a large globe, the type used by schoolchildren everywhere to get some kind of understanding of their place in the world around them — the kind that, in the years of the Empire, showed the British Isles occupying as much space on the planet as India. John would spend hours staring at the countries' names, reading them silently to himself as if reciting a comforting litany. With a finger he'd trace different routes from their home in the north-east of England around the world – to Australia, New Zealand, Canada, imagining himself making those journeys, experiencing for a fleeting moment that thrill of excitement that comes before you set off on an adventure quite outside your usual zone of operations.

He'd take pins and put them in various places that particularly captured his interest, as though by marking them out he could somehow lay claim to them, staking out his territory so that, as the world kept turning, he would not be left behind. Afterwards he'd often reach a new low of despondency as he returned to reality, taking in the oppressive walls, the bolted front door. Trapped within the confines of his own home, to him it seemed impossible that outside there really could exist a world like the one depicted on the globe, where continents led on from continents and seas from seas in a glorious, never-ending technicolor whirl.

One of his pins came to rest securely in Canada. After the letdown of Cyprus and the shambles of Kansas City, the great sprawling mass north of the American border seemed reassuringly civilised and efficient. Not only was English widely spoken and people generally forward-thinking, but it also possessed the kind of natural scenery that most appealed to him – lakes where a man could go out kayaking for a whole day and never get bored, mountains where you could ski in winter and take stunning nature hikes in the summer, forests where a person could hide without fear of being found.

But Canada had three main problems – weather, distance and

a complicated visa requirement procedure. Plus, it was full of expat Brits, which would mean that he would never be quite free to relax. Lost in thought, he spun the globe, letting his finger rest lightly on its spinning surface, feeling it gradually slow down before coming to a halt. For a few seconds he sat there with his eyes closed, like a blind man feeling the world beneath his fingers, and then slowly he turned his head to see where his finger had come to rest.

South America. The irony of this region being the bolthole of choice for generations of the world's greatest criminals was not lost on him. But as he sat staring intently his focus became fixed on the orange shaded patch on the globe where the bulbous landmass that was the Americas seemed to have been squeezed into a narrow funnel right in the middle. Central America: Belize, Costa Rica, El Salvador, Guatemala, Honduras, Nicaragua and Panama.

Hmmm… Well, as a region it had the disadvantage of the language barrier. But on the other hand this was certainly a good destination for anyone who wanted to make very sure they weren't going to bump into anyone from home. The very names of the countries seemed to carry a thrill of the exotic and the weather was more clement than Canada…

The more he thought about it the more appealing Central America seemed. He was sure the red-tape side of things wouldn't be a problem for anyone with a bit of money to invest and the off-the-beaten-track element of the area appealed to his need to see himself as an adventurer, a boundary pusher, rather than someone who followed the crowd and did as they were expected. People from Seaton Carew might holiday in Cyprus or even Canada, but they did not, on the whole, visit Costa Rica or Honduras. He had a good feeling about this one – now all he had to do was convince Anne.

'Are you crazy? We can't even speak the language!' she protested, her normally mournful brown eyes flashing behind her specs. She was still furious with him about the Kansas City episode. Even though she didn't know exactly what had happened, she was aware there had been another woman involved, and that quite a chunk of money had gone missing, with seemingly nothing to show for it. And then there had been the £1,000 he'd splashed out on a boat they never bought. And now here he was proposing they should drop everything and hop over to Guatemala or El Salvador, or one of those other countries she'd only ever heard about in news reports on hurricanes and people forcibly disappearing (as opposed, she couldn't help thinking, to John, who had disappeared himself quite by choice).

But he wouldn't let it go. John always inclined to stubbornness, but the months of virtual solitary confinement had brought out in him an obsessive streak that was almost impossible to counteract. If you put up one argument he'd come right back with another; if you said no he'd keep on and on at you until you agreed with him. Once he had a thought lodged in his head he had to follow it through, no matter what the objections.

Hunched over the computer, he started researching the different countries of Central America – Belize, Costa Rica, El Salvador, Guatemala, Honduras, Nicaragua and Panama. Just reciting the names in his head made him feel adventurous.

It was, he discovered, a region of huge contrasts in terms of politics, culture and geography. Several of the countries he wrote off right away owing to their economic and social instability. Nicaragua was too poor, El Salvador too dangerous, but there were two places which seemed, the more he found out about them, to fit the bill. Costa Rica, with one coastline fronting the Caribbean Sea and the other the Pacific Ocean, was an obvious choice. After more than a century of almost uninterrupted democratically elected government, it enjoyed a stability quite rare in the region, while the protected rainforest had increasingly become a magnet for tourism.

Panama was also on his shortlist. Literally the gateway between South and Central America, the little country might not have appeared an obvious retirement choice. Known mostly for its canal, through which heavy shipping passed between the Atlantic and the Pacific in an endless stream of tankers and industrial vessels, it bordered with volatile Colombia, which meant that it too had more than its share of violent crime. However, it also boasted a buoyant and fast-developing economy, keen to attract international investors and particularly wealthy foreign retirees, while its stunning coastline and breathtaking wildlife made it an ideal place to set up a project within the tourism industry.

Once again he had a plan. For the next few weeks he threw himself into his research, firing off hundreds of emails to estate agents and repatriation agencies, finding out what was on offer in both countries. Gradually he came to focus more and more exclusively on Panama.

Costa Rica was the more secure of the two options, in terms of having an established tourism trade, but it was also considerably more expensive as a result. But Panama seemed to offer the greatest opportunities. The Panamanian government had long recognised the worth of the so-called silver dollar and offered wealthy expats from America and Europe huge incentives to retire to their country in terms of tax breaks and, crucially for the Darwins, an easing of immigration laws. Crucially, no Briton had ever been extradited from there. Unlike, say Canada or Australia, which, it seemed to the ever-proud John Darwin, you almost had to beg to enter, Panama appeared to actively encourage outsiders to move in. And with most of the incomers being North American, he didn't have to worry too much about the threat of a large expat British community.

'Just look at this one,' he said, thrusting a computer printout under Anne's nose. 'For the price of this house we could buy this place right on the beach. Or this one, with all that land.'

She rolled her eyes to signify she wasn't interested, but somehow she couldn't help glancing at the estate agents' particulars that he kept waving in her face. He was right – they did look spectacular, with their views of perfect palm trees and white-flecked oceans, or exotic jungle scenery. It was incredible what they'd be able to buy with the money from the sale of their two Seaton Carew houses.

The more John talked about Panama the weaker Anne's resolve became. It wasn't just the idea of what they'd be gaining, but also the baggage they'd finally be able to leave behind. With every passing week in the prison that was No. 3 The Cliff, John grew more and more morose and difficult to reach. Literally, he had nothing in his life apart from his wife and his computer, and she worried he was becoming de-socialised. How would he cope with being among people again if he spent much more time holed up on his own?

In addition he was missing his sons. When he'd first reappeared and hadn't realised how long everything would take, he had been adamant the boys couldn't know anything and that it would all 'work itself out' some time in the future. But now he'd realised just how long-term the whole scheme would be and how isolated he had begun to feel, he was experiencing all the more keenly the loss of his connection to his sons.

Sometimes when the boys rang Anne would put them on speakerphone so that he could at least have the pleasure of hearing them speak. As their voices rang out around the room he would gaze off intently into space as if trying to recreate a picture of them to go with the sound. Sometimes they'd tell Anne about a problem they were having.

'It's the kind of thing Dad would have known,' they might sigh.

On those occasions John might grab a piece of paper and start scribbling instructions to Anne, which she'd then pass on to whichever son was speaking, as if it were her own idea. In that way at least he was able to preserve some last vestige of communication with his boys, but those snatched scraps of second-hand contact always left him wanting more.

Somehow he'd imagined that he could remain connected to the boys by eavesdropping on their lives, which, he'd somehow imagined, would stay the same as always, just with a space where he used to be. But instead, gradually they'd evolved new lives that closed over the space once occupied by him. Of course they still talked about him and thought about him, but he was no longer an integral factor in their lives and that knowledge ate away at him. The boys didn't know the John Jones he had become, only the John Darwin he once was; he no longer existed to them in real terms, only as a memory, intangible as the wind, and that was harder to bear than he'd imagined.

After the boys rang he'd always be quieter than normal, lost in thought. At times like those the silences between him and Anne could swell like an overstretched balloon until each would be sure that something surely must burst. It's your own fault, she would think angrily, not even able to look at the shell of her former husband on the other side of the room. You brought all this on yourself.

At least the Panama scheme took his mind off the misery of his situation, she conceded. It gave him the chance to dwell on an experience he could be gaining, rather than always brooding on what he'd lost.

Already he'd started his forward planning by insisting Anne should transfer ownership of the two Seaton Carew houses to their elder son, Mark, in advance of their going on the market. If his idea came off there was likely to be quite a lot of money coming their way – and if he and Anne were to be together it was far better that it wasn't directly linked to her.

'Just tell him it's to do with tax,' he told her. 'He'll understand.'

Even so, when John started pressing Anne to commit to a holiday in Central America, she dragged her sensibly shod feet. It was one thing going off to Cyprus for a week, but what would people think about her taking off on her own to Panama for a holiday? She'd never done anything like that before; it would seem so suspicious. Besides, agreeing to the holiday would be like giving the green light to his Panama schemes, which, frankly, grew crazier by the second. One time a hotel, another time a development project, and now he'd come up with this new plan for an activity centre. Some days living with John was like being with Walter Mitty — so busy leading his fantasy lives he totally forgot his real one.

But he was inspired. Yes, he'd had a few false starts, but now he was absolutely sure this was it. This was the big one, the plan that would vindicate everything they'd been through. In years to come, he was convinced, he'd be able to turn to Anne as they watched the sun going down over their own lake or their own tract of rainforest or beach and say, 'Now do you agree it was worth it? Now do you see why it was the best thing we could have done?'

Some men, cooped up on their own for hours every day with only a computer and an increasingly frosty wife for company, might have turned to pornography to ease their frustrations. But for John Darwin, Panamanian real-estate brochures and estate agents' mail-outs became his obsession of choice. When they arrived through the post in brown envelopes addressed to Anne, he'd pause before opening them, savouring the delicious anticipation, the thrill of knowing they might just contain the information that was going to change their lives for ever. Extracting the glossy pages, with tantalising photos of impossibly green palm trees against implausibly blue skies, he'd raise them towards his face and sniff them, breathing in their intoxicating scent of exotic luxury.

Up The Creek Without a Paddle

He was now convinced Panama, with its open-minded economy and its few-questions-asked approach to investment, held the key to their new lives. Panama, with its beach-front developments and rainforest retreats, mountains and waterways, go-getting cities and secluded resorts, was the ideal place for a couple who wanted to make a splash but leave no trace.

As 2006 plodded on towards summer in a monotonous blur, every day much the same as the one before, John Darwin started to plan his Panamanian getaway in more detail. This time there would be no mistakes.

8
NEXT STOP, PANAMA

Whether it was garden gnomes or major fraud, John Darwin was never happier than when he had a goal. Now he'd set his heart on Panama he was insatiable in his determination to find the perfect spot, the perfect investment opportunity. Once again he became in his own mind John Jones, man of the world, wealthy adventurer. It was, in all truth, a far more satisfying role than John Darwin, reclusive dead man, and his confidence noticeably swelled.

Seeing the change in him, Anne didn't have the heart to puncture his bubble. She decided she would go along with the holiday idea. They'd go over for a couple of weeks, have a look around and then, knowing John, he'd go right off the whole scheme and they'd come home again with no harm done. When it came to informing other people she'd have to come up with some explanation for her sudden intrepidness — perhaps she could say that she'd joined some organised tour group or was meeting up with friends. She'd think of something to tell her sons and colleagues when they wondered why quiet-living, unassuming Anne Darwin, who normally holidayed in one of the more accessible, low-budget airline destinations, was suddenly jetting off to a relatively obscure (in the eyes of Hartlepool, anyway), turbulent region of the world for a fortnight's break in a rainforest or jungle retreat.

Leafing through the growing piles of estate agents' particulars, she could feel some of John's relentless, bludgeoning enthusiasm beginning to rub off on her. The properties all looked so attractive and so, well, foreign, with their lush green foliage and clean, white-rendered walls. Just looking at the photos, she could feel the heavy humidity of the Panamanian air, the squawking of tropical birds overhead. Yes, there could be little harm in going for a holiday. It would give John a break from the grinding routine of life at No. 3, and it would be an escape for her too. The strain of leading a double life – widow on the outside, wife at home – was taking its toll, and the idea that she might soon be relaxing on one of the beaches depicted in the brochures proved remarkably seductive.

But by the time the holiday date came around in July 2006, both of them were having serious doubts as to whether they could actually stand being cooped up together for two weeks without even a cupboard door to dive through when tempers became frayed. Once so alien to her, Anne's outbursts of temper where she flounced out the door, slamming it so hard behind her that the overhang of the porch shook above her head, were becoming increasingly frequent. There was still an ignoble satisfaction to be gained from storming down the front path, knowing John was still trapped in the house, unable to follow suit.

Reduced to creeping in and out of the back entrance, he didn't have recourse to any such dramatic gestures. The faint clicking of the interconnecting door, which used an ingeniously placed coat hook to fasten shut, didn't carry quite the same emotional charge.

Locked in mutual antipathy by the hopelessness of their situation, the couple could hardly bear to be in the same room on account of the resentment stirred up at the sight of each other. It didn't bode well for their fortnight of sun, sea and speculating.

The night before their departure Anne was on edge. Once again she was desperately nervous about flying with John. Not only was there his fake passport to worry about, she was also terrified about leaving from Newcastle Airport.

'What if we bump into someone we know?' she agonised for what seemed to him like the hundredth time that night.

'What are the chances of that?' he replied sharply, his patience as thin as the hair fast receding from the top of his head.

But that didn't stop Anne worrying. She tried to channel her concerns into more practical areas that she could actually do something about. Mark would be dog-sitting, but she needed to be sure she'd left enough food. And had she cancelled the milk? What about the papers too? Keeping busy made it easier to ignore the panic that bubbled under the surface of her thoughts, all the time threatening to rise up and engulf her, sweeping away all reason and common sense. Clutching her 'to do' list as though it were a lifebelt, she set about double-checking the already-ticked tasks on the list. Washing taken in? Insurance policy photocopied?

By the time they got to Newcastle Airport the following day she was a nervous wreck. Despite the fact that she was wearing her usual 'make me instantly invisible' middle-aged woman's outfit of unremarkable casuals in insipid shades of pastel, she had the idea that everyone was looking at her, or more particularly at John.

'I'm sure he knows who you are,' she'd hiss whenever anyone looked even remotely in their direction. And, 'That woman was definitely giving us a funny look.'

Her agitated prattle was doing considerable damage to the 'man of the world' impression John had been hoping to cultivate. By this time he liked to think he'd got travelling off to a fine art, feeling proud of the careless ease with which he boarded and got off planes, as if it were no more exciting than catching a bus, but her visible anxiety was ruining everything. 'Just relax. Do a crossword or something,' he told her crossly.

She fumed. It was easy for him to say relax – he wasn't the one who had everything to lose if anyone rumbled them; he'd lost it all once already. She was the one who'd be in the firing line, she was the one people would point, saying, 'Who'd have thought it?' and 'Still waters run deep' and even that tired old expression, 'There's nowt so queer as folk.' Now it was her reputation that would be in tatters. John, as a dead person, technically had no reputation to destroy.

Sucking violently on a boiled sweet from one of the round tins she liked to buy at airports to stop her ears popping on the flight, and checking she had on her special flight socks to guard against blood clots, Anne tried to affect a nonchalance that she was a long way from feeling. All the time John could sense her nervous outrage burning through his lightweight travelling jacket.

Tensions eventually began to thaw out somewhere over the English Channel, en route to catching a connecting flight in Paris. Staying angry was such an effort when you were actually rather excited to be getting away, and when you were quite enjoying the novelty of sitting in public next to your spouse. For the first time in weeks they began to chat to each other in calm, measured tones, without their voices becoming raspy with rage, or rising up at the end of their sentences in ill-disguised recrimination.

John had arranged a busy itinerary of places to visit to make the most of every minute of their two-week stay, and so as the plane ploughed its course steadily across the Atlantic and Anne obediently executed the foot exercises people with bad circulation are advised to do on long-haul flights, they started talking again about the properties they were going to see and got out the well-thumbed estate agents' details to remind themselves which one was which.

For days Anne had passed her eyes over them without really seeing them, just replying, 'It's OK,' or 'That's quite nice,' whenever John asked her what she thought. It was a passive-aggressive way of punishing him, she now belatedly realised. For the first time she really looked at them and was struck by the space you could get for your money and the way all the properties seemed to be flooded with natural light.

Hearing John talk too quickly, as he did whenever he was excited, about the potential of each different place, and seeing the way the stress lines that at home seemed permanently etched into his face were slowly dissolving away, she began to think for the first time in months that there might be a light at the end of the tunnel after all.

Maybe, just maybe, things were starting to go right.

Panama did indeed turn out to be a new beginning for the beleaguered couple. Not only were they free of the oppressive, suffocating fear of discovery which lay over them like freshly dug soil, working its way into every crease and fold of their lives, but the very foreignness of this tropical country gave them the intoxicating sense of having left their old selves far behind.

Even though July is smack in the middle of the Panamanian rainy season, the rains when they came were intense, but passed very quickly, giving way to warm, humid weather that soothed John's light-deprived skin. Everywhere they looked there were sights to exclaim over – wild, exuberant plants they'd never seen before, beaches that looked as if they'd been copied straight from a holiday brochure and the most spectacular array of wild birds – nearly a thousand species, they learned, more than in any other country of the region.

'It's so different,' Anne would gasp on seeing another vividly coloured bird swoop overhead, or another plant, so wildly exotic it seemed impossible that it hadn't found its way off the set of a science-fiction movie.

From England John had got in touch with a relocation agency which had arranged places for them to stay and provided them with a base from which to explore the various properties on their books.

Next Stop, Panama

Bizarrely, despite having been forced together almost 24 hours a day in Seaton Carew, they felt during those first days and nights away as though they were discovering each other afresh, a new couple alone for the first time. As they travelled around the tiny country, traversable in some places by a two-hour car journey from the Atlantic coast to the Pacific, they began to get more of a sense of the geography of the place, and a feel for what they might be able to do there.

John, as usual, was full of schemes that changed as quickly as the unpredictable Panamanian weather. 'I really like the idea of that rainforest guesthouse,' he'd say in the morning, but by the afternoon it might have changed to: 'A place in the city would give us so many options.'

After a few days it occurred to them that they might just be able to manage both — a small flat in the city and a project of some kind on the coast or in the mountains that would provide them with both an income and a way of filling their time.

The relocation company showed them a few options in Panama City itself — a dynamic, if sometimes schizophrenic metropolis torn between embracing the future, with its modern tower blocks and burgeoning business district, and clinging to the past, with the crumbling grand old buildings in the Casco Viejo. Taken as a whole, it wasn't the most attractive city they'd ever visited, but it had the energy and buzz of a place unmistakably on the up, as well as a truly impressive natural park practically on the doorstep. And for the Darwins Panama City offered two enormous additional attractions — it was very cheap and it had a relatively small British expat population.

Up The Creek Without a Paddle

The boss of the relocation company was more than happy to point out the delights of the capital, his hometown. Mario Vilar was well versed in showing nervous middle-aged couples around Panama City. His company, Move to Panama, offered a full relocation service for anyone looking to emigrate, but his clients tended to be mostly early retirees, lured by the climate and the financial incentives on offer to even moderately wealthy 'silver spenders'.

The pale, balding man with his short-sleeved, stay-pressed shirt and his grey-haired wife, her shoulders already pink from unaccustomed exposure to the sun, were no different from hundreds of other potential customers Mario had dealt with over the years. Certainly they were not entirely at ease and the husband had a tendency to talk a lot, probably to cover up his nerves, but then in his experience that was quite normal. After all, many of these people were about to take the greatest gamble of their lives, leaving behind ordered, settled lives to start again in a country where everything was different. Little wonder they looked around with eyes wide with excitement and fear, and took endless photos on little digital cameras bought just for the occasion, to pore over in the comfort of their own living rooms when they got home.

The Joneses had obviously done a lot of research, Mario decided. The man in particular seemed knowledgeable about all the different regions of Panama and the types of real estate available. The woman was quieter, gazing up at her husband from behind her glasses, the expression in her large, brown eyes quite impossible to read.

Sometimes Mario came across couples where one of the two

was obviously far keener on the move than the other. In those cases the partner who was the driving force would take over completely, asking questions and exclaiming loudly as if their own exaggerated interest might somehow compensate for their partner's lack of it. But this pair weren't like that. The woman was thoughtful and reserved, but she didn't seem reluctant. And when she'd shaken Mario's hand her smile had been warm and genuine, lighting up her pinched-looking face as if someone had held a candle up to her chin. And yet there was something about the quality of her silence that made you wonder if maybe they'd argued that morning before setting out, or if she was already missing her family back home in England and doubting whether she really had the nerve to go through with this insane adventure.

The company had sorted the Joneses out with somewhere to stay in the impressive modern business district of El Cangrejo while they looked round the city. When they met in the Move to Panama office one morning, Mario asked Anne and John, as he did all his clients, if they'd mind posing for a photo to go on the company website. Over the years he had found that uncertain customers were comforted by the sight of pictures of others who looked reassuringly similar to them and were going through the same nerve-racking process. The website featured pages of photos of smiling, satisfied customers posing awkwardly in newly acquired apartments, or hugging the pet dogs that his firm had helped import into the country.

Occasionally you found people objected, either because they didn't like having their photo taken or they weren't happy with it being used. But John Jones and his wife didn't seem bothered at all. In fact they were most accommodating, smiling broadly for the camera alongside Mario in his usual work outfit – smart shirt (in this case, blue and white vertical stripes) tucked into smart-casual jeans. As always, the date would appear automatically stamped across the picture: 14/7/2006.

But Anne and John didn't pay the photo a second thought as they made their way back to their lodgings. It was a small company in Central America. How many people would ever see that picture? And it wasn't as if they were using their real names. No, as they walked along the bustling city streets, their conversation was all about Panama itself. Though they hadn't yet seen anything they wanted to buy, both had warmed to the country, with its easygoing charm and stunning scenery. Anne still couldn't quite get to grips with the idea of living there full time, of waking up in the morning to blazing sunshine and the sound of the tropical birds outside, but it was as if, at least while she was there, she was willing to suspend disbelief and join in John's fantasy world, where they were a couple of ageing trailblazers, looking around the country they were about to call home.

She was even prepared to take the first step in the property-buying process. They'd discovered that in Panama it was common practice for foreigners to purchase a property through a shell company set up by themselves, rather than as individuals. In this way they need never disclose their names. No doubt there were tax benefits in doing so, but for the publicity-shy Darwins this was a double blessing. They could become property owners without ever being officially identified. And so they decided to set up a company with their sons as shareholders – that way the boys would benefit from any future profits.

'Any ideas on a company name?' Anne asked, flustered now things seemed to be moving so quickly and, as usual, happy to hand over all responsibility to her husband. Never one for the off-the-cuff remark or impulsive decision, John took this kind of thing very seriously, eventually coming up with the name Jaguar, one of Panama's six indigenous species of wild cat. To be honest, neither of them could still quite believe they would shortly be living in a country where such animals roamed free. It was so impossibly exotic for the quiet-living couple from Cleveland.

As their two-week stay in Panama finally drew to a close they prepared, with hearts as heavy as their over-stuffed cases, to head back to Seaton Carew. It wasn't just end-of-holiday blues – that creeping realisation that the real life you've held at bay for the past few days or weeks is still waiting for you just round the corner, exactly as it was when you left – for the Joneses, aka the Darwins, the end of the fortnight also meant an end to life as a normal couple.

In Panama they could stop off for a coffee at any one of the pavement cafés without fear of being spotted. They could shop together, eat together and even leave their room together, just like any other normal couple. For John, after years of sneaking out the back door under cover of darkness, it was a thrill to stroll up to the door at the end of a morning's house-hunting, or an evening out, to take the key from his pocket and walk inside the house, not even checking behind him to see if anyone was looking.

They'd hardly argued at all during their stay. After so much time with each leading a life that was completely separate from the other, and from which the other was completely excluded, Panama had brought them together again. Every new experience was one they shared; every time they saw a new kind of scenery or ate something they'd never tried before, this united them in a sense of mutual appreciation. It wasn't quite a second honeymoon, but at least they were being kind to each other.

'I wish we didn't have to go back,' Anne sighed over dinner on their last night in Panama.

'Soon we won't have to,' said John. 'We'll go home, put the houses on the market, and this time next year we'll be living here for good. Trust me.'

She glanced over at him sharply, trying to read his expression in the faltering light of the balmy Panamanian evening, but she could already tell any irony was completely lost on him. This was the man who'd faked his own death, who'd made her lie to their sons, who'd gone to America chasing some fantasy woman from the Internet and had lost them a fortune as a result. And now here he was telling her to trust him.

But the truly maddening thing was, she almost did.

The next morning, as the Darwins made their way to the airport on the first leg of their long journey home, Mario Vilar uploaded a batch of photos from his camera on to his computer. Here were all the clients he'd been dealing with over the past couple of weeks. Systematically captioning each one with the first names of the people in the photo, together with the service the company had carried out for them, he gave each picture a quick appraisal. When he came to the photo of the smiling Joneses he hardly registered it at all, apart from to note how Anne's teeth looked more prominent than they had in real life and to make a mental note to himself not to smile quite so cheesily next time.

When they were all labelled, he pressed the key to add them to the page of client photos already on the company website. It was a little extra work for him, he thought, but it never hurt to have pictures of happy customers on the site. Besides, one day he might just be glad he'd kept this running record of the people who passed through his offices.

It always paid to think ahead because, as he was forever reminding customers, you never knew what was around the corner.

9
SELLING UP

A nyone wishing to ease themselves gently back into real life after a foreign holiday would be well advised not to attempt to go straight from tropical Central America to Hartlepool, recently named one of the UK's 20 Worst Places to Live.

Getting back into the same numbing routine felt doubly cruel to John after the freedom he'd enjoyed in Panama. No sooner had he slipped in through the back door after their return from the airport than he felt the oppressive weight of enforced confinement settle over him like a lumpy quilt. It was all right for Anne – she still had her work to go off to and family to visit. It was he who was trapped in a lofty-ceilinged netherworld where daylight never quite seemed to filter through the net curtains; it was he who had to watch his holiday suntan fading before his eyes in the gloom of yet another disappointing summer's day. The only vague light on the horizon was the plan that had slowly begun to form during their two-week getaway: sell up and ship out.

Anne had started selling off some of the other houses in their portfolio a couple of years before, but now that they were about to put the Seaton Carew properties on the market he started to notice all the things that needed doing to them. Those lucky enough to own a seafront home will know only too well the damage that the elements can inflict on outside window frames and doors, and the inside had fared little better. Two enormous properties like 3 and 4 The Cliff require endless upkeep and everywhere John looked it seemed there was peeling paint or cracked plaster, or even small patches of old damp.

He had occasionally done the odd job on the rental properties they owned. Even while in hiding he'd ventured out a few times to try to and fix a toilet or leaking pipe. Strangely, the cunning disguises he adopted on these occasions seemed designed to attract rather than deflect attention. Sometimes it would be the bushy beard and woolly hat combo, which he might finish off with a boiler suit, and the ubiquitous limp.

One tenant could hardly tear her eyes away from the very obvious bushy brown wig the odd-job man was sporting under his flat cap. Whatever his appearance it must be said that he hadn't exactly impressed anyone with his handiwork, with Anne often receiving a phone call a few days later complaining about a bodge.

But doing odd jobs provided John with a new focus. It took his mind off the soul-destroying monotony of his daily life and made him feel as if he was at least doing something to hasten the fulfilment of their goal. Now, when Anne came home after a day at work and asked from force of habit what he'd done that day, she didn't just get a one-word answer but a list of things he'd accomplished, little tasks he'd ticked off: the replacing of a damaged section of skirting board, the fixing of a leaky tap. Even so, they realised that selling the two Seaton Carew properties was not going to be easy. Though the UK property market as a whole was buoyant in the second half of 2006, prices in that area of the north-east still lagged way behind the rest of the country and finding a buyer for two such enormous residences was not going to be easy.

Another thing that wasn't easy, at least for Anne, was telling friends about her holiday without mentioning her holiday companion. So many times she was on the point of saying, 'John thought…' or, 'John said…' but then stopped herself just in time. When she flashed round her holiday snaps, making vague mentions of tour guides and groups, and everyone was duly impressed, she was grateful no one thought to ask who'd taken the pictures, or whose wine glass was next to hers on the table.

Meanwhile his conviction that the end was now in sight was making John feel cockier than he'd done in a long while. So cocky in fact that when a neighbouring hotel owner applied for planning permission to make changes to his property he lodged an objection, jauntily signing it in the name of John Jones, No. 4 The Cliff, Seaton Carew.

John Darwin, master meddler, was back on form.

Selling a house is always a pain. First, you have to make it look good, then you have to scurry round cleaning it every time a potential buyer comes round, and then there are the little touches you're forever being told make all the difference – fresh flowers in the hallway, coffee brewing in the kitchen. But if selling a normal house is bad, selling a house divided up into lots of bedsits can be a nightmare. There's never a good time to show people round, never a time when you can be sure the hallways will be clear, the bathrooms empty.

Two thousand and six merged sluggishly into 2007 and still there was no movement. John tried to keep the momentum going from their Panamanian sojourn, but it was hard to carry on contacting estate agents and researching the price of health care and the different types of accounts and interest rates when there was no telling what time frame they might be looking at.

'It'll happen,' Anne tried to be upbeat. 'We've just got to be patient.'

'Easy for you to say,' John growled, scowling at his computer screen.

In private he was starting to wonder whether they'd ever get rid of the houses that had come to symbolise to him the shackles that were holding him back. He and Anne would talk endlessly about what they'd do if they got a low offer and what was their absolute minimum price, but the few prospective buyers who came didn't hang around to discuss prices, perhaps put off by the uncared-for feel of the place – so many doors, so many secrets. Then, in February 2007, they had a lucky break.

Gary Hepple had spotted No. 4 The Cliff on an estate agent's books and thought it sounded like a good investment opportunity, particularly when the agent informed him that the owners were keen to sell and would negotiate on price. But when he and his wife turned up at the appointed time to take a look round there was no sign of life. He'd later describe to a newspaper how, after waiting at the front door, they tried to peer through the window but the view inside was blocked by a set of grubby net curtains.

'After all that, and there's not even anyone here!' he frowned, turning away annoyed and pulling his mobile from his pocket. But just as he was dialling the estate agent's number the front door creaked open. From inside came a gruff male voice: 'If it's a delivery, leave it next door!'

Gary was getting fed up: 'No, I've come to see about the house. The house that's for sale?'

For a few moments there was no reply, and then the voice spoke again: 'Well, I suppose you'd better come inside.'

As welcomes go, it wasn't the most gracious, but then the Hepples had come out of their way to see this house, so they might as well go in. Gary shot his wife a questioning look. Then, shrugging, he led the way back up the path. Nudging the door open apprehensively, he was taken aback to come across a strange, hunched figure in the entrance hallway. The man was leaning on a walking stick and his exaggerated stoop meant that he found himself talking to the top of his woolly hat rather than his face.

When he finally did raise his head the Hepples were surprised to find he wasn't as old as he'd first appeared, but still there was something odd about him. After a few seconds Gary realised what it was: the man never actually looked at him, instead he stared just past him, as if addressing his attention to a point above the doorframe.

The situation was just becoming awkward when a woman

appeared from somewhere else in the house. Small, with hair that seemed somehow shockingly grey, as if it had aged faster than her face, she had a slightly hesitant smile that was a relief after the man's gruff indifference. 'I'm so sorry,' she said in the kind of voice that made them feel she actually meant it. 'I was tied up with something.'

The woman explained that she herself lived next door at No. 3, but she was also the owner of No. 4. They never did quite catch what the strange guy with the stick did, but they assumed he might be a caretaker or even, heaven forbid, a sitting tenant.

The Hepples were slightly taken aback when Anne Darwin, as she'd introduced herself, started showing them round and it became clear that the oddball in the hat would be tagging along too. His limping presence had an inhibiting effect, making them more wary about commenting on the state of the rooms, or the amount of repair work that would be needed – which was, to be frank, considerable.

'I'd be looking to turn it into a guesthouse,' Gary explained to Anne. 'So it'd need a lot of money spending on it.'

Anne shot a quick, questioning glance at the man with the hat and then seemed to come to a decision. 'Make me an offer,' she told the Hepples. 'I'm willing to negotiate for a quick sale.'

Walking away from the house, the Hepples agreed it had been a very bizarre encounter, but they felt the house definitely had potential. 'And she was so quick to come down on money,' Gary speculated. 'Sounds like she's quite desperate to get shot of it.' They decided they'd make her an offer – provided, of course, the man with the woolly hat and the stick and the shifty expression wasn't part of the deal.

Selling Up

When the estate agent rang to tell Anne the Hepples had offered £160,000 for No. 4, she was ecstatic. 'Finally I'll be rid of that millstone around my neck,' she told John, jubilant at the thought of seeing the back of the bedsits, with their never-ending problems of unpaid rent, complaining tenants, leaks and breakages.

John had his own reasons to be happy. No. 4 had come to represent to him all that was most soul-destroying about his life after death – the stale air, the curtains drawn against the light, the endless monotony of days that bled into each other when nothing ever changed. The house had effectively become his own private prison, and knowing that it would soon be sold was like being given a release date. All too late he felt some empathy with the inmates of Holme House Prison, where he'd worked in what seemed like (and technically was, he supposed) another lifetime. Too late he understood how it might feel to build a life around one single solitary mental image – that of your own feet walking out through the prison gate.

In a kind of symbolic gesture he sealed up the secret passageway between the two houses with breezeblocks and hardboard wedged into place with pages torn from a magazine. Later, with the entrance uncovered by the new owners, the magazine was found to be the February edition of *Emigrate Canada*. The sale of No. 4 would take him one step away from his grey, half-lived limbo, and one step closer to realising his Panamanian dream.

To celebrate the Darwins decided to reward themselves with another trip to Panama. This time they'd go in March before the rainy season set in. Now they had a better idea of the country they'd be able to target the areas they were interested in and make far better use of their time. Once again John was in his element – making lists, firing off emails, burning with renewed motivation.

By this time, after the Cyprus trip and the first Panama trip, Anne's friends and family were getting used to this hitherto unsuspected intrepid side of her character and didn't query her breezy announcement that she was making a return visit to the country she'd fallen in love with.

They travelled from Newcastle Airport on the first leg of a journey that would see them changing airlines in Paris and Venezuela. Once again, when the day of departure dawned, Anne was petrified they'd be spotted and insisted on leaving the house early in the morning while it was still dark. The whole of the first part of the journey she was unable to relax, digging the sensibly short nails of one hand into the palm of the other in an effort not to betray how nervous she really was.

'It'll be fine,' John told her almost boastfully. 'I've done this loads of times. No one's going to stop me.'

Nevertheless, it wasn't until they'd taken off from Paris that she felt able to start unwinding and actually began to get excited about their trip. Through a relocation agency John had arranged for them to stay with a host family in Panama City when they arrived. Anne had had major misgivings when she'd first found out – John wasn't always the easiest of people to get on with at first acquaintance. Nor, it had to be said, at second or third acquaintance.

But staying with a local family proved an unexpected pleasure. Not only because they were living with native Panamanians, who treated them with such old-fashioned courtesy and warmth, but also because they were able to interact with other people as a couple once more, rather than as two separate individuals united by a secret both were trying desperately to forget. John loved the feeling of being part of Panamanian life, not just going to the usual tourist haunts, ticking off the predictable sights in a generic guidebook. Every time they'd ever been on holiday he'd been the same, keen to distance themselves from the rest of the holiday hordes, to demonstrate that the Darwins weren't like 'all the other tourists', but a class apart who ate the local food and even tried to master a few words in the local language.

Giddy with the prospect of getting £160,000 from the sale of their home, they threw themselves into house-hunting, spending their days scouring the areas they'd earmarked the last time they were there, traipsing in and out of air-conditioned apartment blocks, John using a hankie to mop his balding pate if the heat became too much. Their initial requirements were modest: they wanted a small flat in Panama City itself. Ideally it would have two bedrooms so their sons could visit Anne and a large balcony from which to enjoy the sunshine. Oh, and they didn't want an area with too many British tourists or resident expats.

'We want to integrate into the local community,' John explained haughtily to the estate agent who was showing them round. The estate agent smiled. Fast becoming a mecca for well-off emigrants from the States and Europe, the country was full of people wanting to find the real Panama, not appreciating that it was as elusive as the mercury in the outside thermometers, changing with each new wave of incomers, each new boost in tourism.

You'd think it would be easy for a couple who'd spent the past few years residing in their own private hell to find something they liked. Surely anything would seem like an improvement? And yet, when the world is suddenly your oyster, the responsibility of choice can weigh heavily. Certainly John Darwin found it so. After all those lost years, that shadowy, twilight existence back in Hartlepool, Panama was to be his nirvana and he was determined that it should match his exacting expectations.

Incredibly, they at last found somewhere he was happy with. It was in the fortuitously named area of El Dorado – literally meaning 'the gilded one' and suggesting a place of fabulous wealth. This was a quiet, somewhat run-down suburb of Panama City, mostly notable for its shopping mall and proximity to the city's famous Metropolitan Natural Park, a huge area of protected land containing a forest and several threatened species of wildlife, all within the capital's perimeters. And it was available to move into immediately.

The flat itself was small, but immaculately furnished, with all the furniture and fittings included in the £40,000 price tag. It had a large, bright living room, a terrace that was a real suntrap and new outside furniture on which to lounge and enjoy far-reaching views across the city to the distant sea. The kitchen boasted modern wooden units, while the white walls were broken up with several ceramic sculptures showing the face of the sun. For a couple used to living behind net curtains in a part of the world where it routinely grows dark at 3pm in winter, and where summers can seem to drift past without a break in the clouds, it was like a different world.

Now they had their city base it was time to set in motion the next step in their long-term plan – finding a business venture to fund their Panamanian dream. John Darwin, as has already been seen, was something of an outdoors enthusiast. He was a keen walker and cyclist, but what he liked to do above all else was to paddle kayaks. With its lakes and beaches and deserted tropical islands, Panama was a paradise for anyone with an interest in water sports. And with its relatively young but fast-expanding tourism industry and injection of foreign investment, it was quickly gaining a reputation for its eco-resorts – places where so-called 'responsible' holidaymakers could relax in the knowledge that their pleasure-seeking wasn't doing anything to harm the local environment and was, wherever possible, helping sustain it.

The idea that had formed in John's mind was to open a tourist resort catering for kayak and canoe enthusiasts. If the thought ever struck him that a man who'd gone paddling out to sea on the stillest of spring days and never come back wasn't perhaps the best qualified to be running canoeing holidays, it was soon dismissed. As far as he was concerned it was the ideal occupation. He would be outside, doing what he loved best, and imparting the wisdom of his experience to other people. What could be wrong with that?

Anne wasn't so sure, though. '*Kayaking* holidays?' she queried, doubt etched into every crease of her face. 'Are you quite sure that's...?'

But John didn't even let her finish, so utterly convinced was he that this was the way forward, and so keen to win her over to his way of thinking. 'It's absolutely perfect. We've got the flat here in town that's near all the banks and shops and restaurants, then we can buy some land in the middle of nowhere and run the tourist resort from there. We'd really have the best of both worlds.'

145

Up The Creek Without a Paddle

As usual she eventually found herself agreeing with him, despite the little voice inside her jumping up and down and screaming, 'Hang on...'

Later, when her husband had dropped off to sleep, she mulled over the whole ridiculous, crazy plan. At the age of 55, when most of her contemporaries were waiting out their working lives until retirement, or knitting blankets for their grandchildren, she was about to ditch her receptionist job, move thousands of miles away and run an outdoor pursuits resort in the blazing heat – and all this without raising any eyebrows back home?

John had no such misgivings. Through an estate agent they went to look at various plots of land and within days they'd found what they were looking for. Villa Escobal was a 194-hectare plot of rainforest on the banks of Lake Gatún, once the largest man-made body of water in the world and now home to a rich diversity of wildlife. The land itself carried a price tag of £195,000 and an ambitious purchaser would have to put up the same again if they wanted to build a hotel with access to the lake. Typical of John, he listened seriously to the agent's patter without betraying any sign of anxiety, for all the world as if he threw sums like that around all the time.

Just from looking at him, Anne could tell that John had already fallen in love with the breathtaking scenery and had already envisaged himself as the host of a small but smart hotel peopled by outdoor enthusiasts like him. When he started to describe how they could install a cable car to get guests from the hotel to the lake she knew it was all over. Even so, she still felt duty bound to try to raise objections. 'But it's such a massive undertaking,' she said half-heartedly.

Selling Up

Even before the words were out of her mouth she knew it was a waste of time. John had that closed look in his eyes that meant he'd already made up his mind. And, as she looked around again, she had to admit it was stunningly beautiful, with its jungles and long green grass, and so isolated – they'd feel perfectly safe here from curious passers-by who happened to know too much.

She imagined herself and John building a life in that verdant, unspoilt wilderness. They'd spend their days fishing or riding horses; they'd even grow their own vegetables, or live off fruit from the trees that grew everywhere there – mangoes, oranges, limes and plums. Before she really knew what was happening she found she'd agreed to buy, not only the flat in Panama City but also Finca Escobal.

The Darwins' Panamanian property portfolio was born.

Now John powered into action. With the sales agreed there was important paperwork to be sorted out, and he was just the man to do it. Already they'd set up their shell company, Jaguar Properties Corporation, the previous year and so they were able to proceed relatively quickly, but as with any property purchases, nothing was quite so simple as it appeared – all sorts of odds and ends would need to be sorted out.

In between phone calls to banks and meetings with lawyers the Darwins talked about what they would do next. The answer was blindingly obvious. 'I'll stay here,' John announced. 'I'll stay in a hotel while I'm overseeing the property purchases, and then move into the flat as soon as it's all gone through.'

As soon as the words were out of his mouth Anne could see how much sense it made. He was desperate not to go back to the UK, and here was the perfect excuse to stay on in the place that was already far more like home to him than their rambling Hartlepool house had ever been. And if she were honest it would be quite a relief for her to go back there on her own. It would be so much easier to play the part of the brave, intrepid widow determined to embark on the adventure of a lifetime, without the inhibiting presence of her decidedly alive husband through the partition wall. In the meantime, or so John's plan went, Anne would return home and try to sell No. 3 The Cliff as quickly as possible. Then it was just a question of packing up all their stuff and her moving over to join him. 'In a few months the whole nightmare will be over,' he told her confidently.

But the more she thought about it the more she couldn't help thinking that while John's nightmare might well be over, her own could just be about to get worse. While she was relieved that he wouldn't be coming back to Seaton Carew to resume the mind-numbing half-life that had slowly been driving them both crazy, she was daunted by the task ahead of her – having to single-handedly pack up their house and oversee all the arrangements. Not to mention coming up with a plausible story for colleagues and family as to why, after all these years of dull respectability, she was suddenly giving up everything and moving to the tropics.

Gosh, what if they thought she was one of those sad menopausal Shirley Valentine women she was always reading about in the papers, who gave up perfectly good lives to live in a hut on a beach with a toy boy who was only after them for their money? It didn't bear thinking about.

The last night together was about as emotionally charged as a couple not given to lavish displays of affection were likely to get. John had booked himself into the Costa Inn, a popular but inexpensive hotel in the La Exposicion area of the city, busy enough that he could be assured of remaining anonymous.

'You'll be fine,' he told Anne, reading the cause of her nervousness without having to be told. 'It's all going to come together for us now, I can feel it.'

Those words echoed in her about-to-pop ears as her plane started its descent through the clouds towards Newcastle Airport. Everything was going to go right now. The nightmare was over.

Ever seen those films where someone wakes up from a bad dream and realises it's all been a dream, but just as relief floods through them it turns out that bit is also part of the nightmare, which is ongoing and has never actually stopped? Had Anne Darwin been a more fanciful kind of woman she might well have remembered seeing scenes like that and perhaps been slightly less willing to believe in the existence of fresh starts and second chances.

Sometimes what looks like a brave new world turns out to have been built on the diseased foundations of the old one.

10
OUR MAN IN PANAMA

ack in England Anne didn't waste any time in getting No. 3 on
the market. Being a single-unit family home, this house was
in far better shape than the one next door and consequently
commanded a heftier price tag.

Now that they were already committed to the Panama Plan she
was anxious to get on with it. Already Seaton Carew no longer felt
like home. The house, with its For Sale sign outside, seemed like
someone else's home when she pulled up outside it after a day at
work. Whenever she let herself into the big, empty hall it felt
almost as if she was an intruder. She occupied the rooms
apologetically, like a house-sitter never quite at home.

Few people were surprised when she told them that she was
selling up. For years they'd been asking themselves what one
widow was doing rattling round in a seven-bedroom house. It was
generally assumed she'd be moving somewhere smaller – a nice

little bungalow with a manageable tidy garden perhaps, or maybe down south nearer her sons. So when Anne started to let slip, as casually as she could, that she was thinking of spending some time in Panama, you could almost hear the collective intake of breath. There was a certain unwritten code of behaviour that all widows were expected to accept unquestioningly – they were required to quietly pack up their houses, send surplus belongings to Oxfam in neatly tied bin bags and then move to sensibly proportioned accommodation near to their friends or family, with modern kitchens that needed very little cleaning, and take up voluntary work to fill up their spare time. Widows did not start new lives in rainforests.

'She's very brave,' people would whisper in tones that quite clearly meant almost the opposite, that she must be mad. But few told her so to her face. She'd be back, they assured one another, when it all went wrong.

Her sons were naturally worried. When your recently widowed mother suddenly announces she's planning to turn her back on everything she knows and start a new life in a far-off tropical country, it's bound to cause concern. But they knew how much she'd enjoyed her visits there, and when she showed them the brochures and guide books piled high in the office they realised this wasn't some half-baked impulse scheme. She'd done her research and, more than that, the idea seemed to have animated her in a way she hadn't shown in years. This could be just the new start she needed.

At first there was little serious interest in the house. Most people don't have call for seven bedrooms unless they've an unusually large family or are willing to spend megabucks to turn it into a hotel.

Meanwhile Anne carried on with her everyday life, going into the Gilesgate Medical Centre in Durham as she'd done for years, chatting with patients and colleagues, answering the phone in her usual friendly, efficient manner. 'Well, he's completely booked up today, but let me just see if I can squeeze you in,' she'd soothe anxious mothers and flu-ridden pensioners.

Inside she felt a growing impatience to be gone. It was as if her body was here in Hartlepool – dutifully trudging into work, making endless cups of tea for the other staff and smiling apologetically at patients whose appointments were running late – but her mind was back in Panama, sipping coffee at pavement cafés while emerald-coloured parrots flew overhead.

Ironically, now that she and John were no longer trapped together under the same roof they talked more than ever before – long phone calls and emails in which they discussed at length how the purchase of the flat in Panama City was progressing and who, if anyone, had come to view the house. He seemed particularly concerned by something he'd heard about changes to visa regulations in Panama. Anne couldn't be completely sure she'd understood him properly – sometimes when it came to money and bureaucracy she found herself feeling just like one of the schoolchildren he used to teach, as he tried with increasingly ill-disguised exasperation to explain something to her. As far as she could gather he'd found out that he wouldn't be able to remain in Panama on a tourist visa, as he'd first thought. Instead they'd need an investor's visa, which would entail their identities being verified

153

by the British police. He seemed to think that the only way to get past this was for him to revert to being John Darwin again.

Anne wasn't quite sure how he intended to do this, and right then she didn't want to know either – she had enough on her plate tying up all the loose ends in the UK without fretting about what might happen when she got to Panama. Instead of thinking about all the things that could go wrong, she tried to concentrate on the ones that were at last going right – like the changes she'd noticed in her husband, for example.

Released from his Seaton Carew captivity, John was a different person – full of news of things that had happened and people he'd met, as well as his usual, ever-fluid plans for their future. His emails were arrogant and flirty, revealing a return to the John of old. 'Well, you sexy beast,' read one, which would later be recovered by Sky News and read out to an enthralled courtroom. 'I'm standing out on the balcony in the nudy, typing this for you. Just hope the mosquitoes or other bugs don't bite, or at least not in a certain place – don't want it all lumpy!' Another, also later handed over by Sky News to be used in the police investigation into the Darwins, jokingly referred to Anne as a 'filthy rich gringo'.

After the years of pitying her husband's self-imposed confinement, she now envied him his freedom. It seemed to her that he was already starting the adventure without her and she listened to descriptions of his day with a mixture of fascination and frustration.

For John, the man who'd already been reborn once, this period in Panama offered yet another opportunity for reinvention. From being a non-person hiding away behind grubby net curtains, he was now striding around a capital city in a country where humming birds swarmed round trees teaming with sloths, an area of volcanic mountains and rainforests. Slowly he was learning to speak Spanish and never failed to get a thrill of satisfaction when he went into a shop and ordered, say, a white coffee with a pastry and got, yes, a white coffee with a pastry.

In his smart, short-sleeved shirts and crease-free khaki shorts, John Darwin trod the streets of Panama City, gradually learning his way from one area to the next. This was to be his home and he was determined to master its layout, getting to know all the streets, markets, bars and plazas. Already he knew the best places to hide his money in case of mugging and which cash machines charged commission. He cut, he liked to think, quite a striking figure as he strode purposefully round the city, attending meetings with bank managers, lawyers and estate agents; he was at last a man in charge of his own destiny: Our Man in Panama.

After about five weeks in the Costa Inn the paperwork on both the El Dorado apartment and the Escobal project was finally in order, with the money having been processed through Jaguar Properties. The rainforest resort would have to go on the back burner until the other Seaton Carew property was sold, but the apartment was ready to move into straightaway. Carrying his suitcase through the lobby of the hotel he'd called home for the past month, John was both excited and apprehensive. This really was it now. The adventure started here.

Put yourself in the position of John Darwin as he made his way across town, with the sun beating down through the window of the taxi. Everywhere he looked was a hive of activity with people doing all kinds of things that were, unmistakably, thrillingly, foreign. He was about to take possession of a new home with a view across a dynamic, modern-thinking city and soon he would have access to a substantial amount of money with which to fund a business venture in an activity he was passionate about. Even better, he had taken on the system, paying what had seemed at times to be an intolerable price, but now he was about to reap the rewards. Could life have seemed much sweeter?

The apartment that he and Anne had chosen, which tabloid newspapers would later refer to as a 'penthouse', was in fact a modest, fourth-floor apartment in a terracotta-and-white painted block in a safe but rather shabby district of the city. True, the block was fronted by a tall, graceful palm tree, reaching almost to the Darwins' balcony, which lent an air of instant exoticism, but it was also situated on a busy bottleneck, from where the noise of horns blaring and drivers yelling drifted up throughout the day.

To John, however, so recently used to being incarcerated inside the four gloomy walls of his curtained house, the apartment was ideal. He could come and go at any time he liked, without checking first to see if anyone else was around. And he could say hello to other neighbours he met in the lobby or the lift without instinctively averting his eyes to forestall any attempts at conversation. For the first time in years he was able to make himself fully at home, spreading himself like butter around the compact apartment, luxuriating in the fact that it didn't matter if he left traces, that he didn't have to clear up after himself so that, seconds after leaving a room, no one could tell he had ever been there.

With Anne away he made the most of having the flat to himself, covering its surfaces with sticky labels identifying each object – chair, table or cupboard – with its Spanish name.

'*Silla*,' he'd pronounce carefully, before sitting down on a chair.

'*Mesa*,' he'd recite, putting his cup down on the table.

But he wasn't the kind of man who would be content sitting with his feet up on the sofa reading a whodunit. Now that they'd bought the land on Lake Gatún he was anxious to start getting the building work underway; nor was he deterred by the fact that the house in Seaton Carew wasn't yet sold. He was convinced it was just a matter of time.

'Come over for a few weeks,' he entreated Anne. 'Let's get everything in motion.'

'I don't know if I can get so much time off,' she would demur down the phone long distance from her study in No. 3, where she was trying to master reflexive verbs from her *Teach Yourself Spanish* textbook. But the fact was she was looking forward to getting back to Panama. Now that they had their own flat there she was anxious to get settled and start buying a few bits and pieces to make it seem more like home.

As a highly regarded member of staff she was able to persuade her bosses to allow her a six-week holiday. Everyone knew that Anne Darwin had been through a lot over the past few years, and no one was going to deny her some time off if it would help in her recovery. Amazed at her own daring, she booked a return flight to Panama in July 2007, just three months after her last visit.

Up The Creek Without a Paddle

This time the anxiety that marred her previous flights with John was absent and she was free to savour the excitement of the journey, spending hours in the book shops at the airport departure lounge, debating which magazines to choose to see her through the long flight and stocking up on extra sun cream and insect repellent in the chemist's. Whenever she gained her seat on each leg of the journey she didn't keep her eyes trained on the ground so as to discourage her neighbours from chatting, but instead smiled warmly, inviting conversation. For the first time she felt like she was going on a proper holiday – the kind where you get to relax and forget about your real life and send people postcards listing all the books you've managed to read and how high the temperatures soared the day before.

When John came to meet her at the airport just outside Panama City she felt almost as if the past few nightmare years had never happened and they were a normal couple reunited after a long separation.

'You look well,' she told him almost shyly. And it was true that, with his deep tan and his new air of confidence, John seemed to be glowing with health and barely concealed enthusiasm.

'Just wait until I show you...' he told her about a hundred times that night, almost school-boyish in his eagerness to demonstrate what he'd been doing while she'd been gone.

Anne wondered at the change in him. She was so used to feeling sorry for him, or just plain irritated by him, but this was the John she'd known years ago – the one who made decisions and took charge, and was knowledgeable and impressive. Had she been a Mills & Boon type of woman Anne Darwin might have described it as almost like falling in love all over again.

Our Man in Panama

The six weeks in Panama turned out to be almost magical. With John's headstart he'd already found out the best places to buy food or go for a coffee, and he'd proudly show her around as if he were a native rather than a tourist himself.

'I always buy my newspaper from here in the mornings,' he'd tell her. Or, 'This is the best place to watch the sunset.'

For a while Anne was puzzled about the subtle shift in her feelings, not knowing how to identify the source of her newfound contentment with her late husband. Then, one day as he was explaining something about his ideas for the resort, she suddenly realised what it was: respect. Ever since John had shuffled back into her life, grubby, unkempt and with nowhere else to go, she'd looked after him, pitied him, often been irritated by him, sometimes even hated him, but this was the first time in ages that she'd been able to respect him, and it felt really good.

For his part, if John had ever been happier, for the life of him he certainly couldn't remember it. Over the past five years there had been times, he didn't mind admitting now, when he'd had serious doubts about whether he hadn't made the biggest and most stupid mistake ever that day back in 2002 when he'd stood looking out to sea and decided it was a good day to become dead.

But now, sitting on the balcony of his Panama City flat, sipping chilled white wine while the setting sun stained the white apartment blocks in different shades of pink and orange, he knew it had all been worth it. Back in England the relentless demands of their ever-growing debt would have ground them both down to nothing in the end, gradually stripping them of all they'd built up, all that made them the people they were.

He'd have had to admit defeat to the world. All those people he'd bragged to about his property portfolio and his two enormous seafront houses would have liked nothing better than to gather to watch the bailiffs pecking away like malicious magpies at their possessions. After all his fine talk about becoming a millionaire he and Anne would have been reduced to nobodies, dependent on the charity of the state.

But now, five years later, here was vindication of everything he'd done. The faint whisper of the breeze through the palm trees, the rainbow arcing across a suddenly clear sky to celebrate the end of a short-lived downpour, the deeply etched worry-lines miraculously smoothed from Anne's lightly tanned face. All this was proof that he'd done the right thing, the noble thing. He'd taken the kind of risk another man might only have dreamed of, and held on fast to it, where another might have cracked under the strain. Who dares wins, the motto goes. Well, John Darwin had dared and now, it was fair to say, he had won.

Looking out across his new kingdom from his fourth-floor castle, he allowed himself the luxury of self-congratulation. He alone had accomplished this; he alone had pulled it off. Others in his situation might have allowed themselves to be bent and broken by the system, accepting as inevitable the painful spiral into debt, but he had looked for the other way.

For those who dare there is always another way.

Panama has long been one of the more overlooked of the Central and South American nations. It lacks the glamour of Brazil, the epic scale of Peru or Argentina or the lingering scent of tragedy of

Our Man in Panama

El Salvador or Nicaragua. Sandwiched between high-profile Costa Rica to the north and Colombia, with its international reputation for drug-related violence to the south, it has long been dismissed by many as 'Bland-ama', a country with few attractions apart from tax exemption and the fact that a burgeoning over-fifties immigrant population made it unlikely anyone would ever want for a bridge partner.

But John Darwin loved it, and not just because you could open an offshore bank account without giving a name, or because you didn't pay tax on any income earned outside of the country, or even because anyone over 45 with a monthly income of over £200 or more was welcomed with open arms. No, while those might have been factors in attracting him in the first place, the reason he had come to love Panama was because it was his – he had researched it and he had founded and funded it. He hadn't arrived expecting to slot into a ready-made expat community, he hadn't come under the shelter of a tour group or a company relocation scheme; he and Anne had come without introduction or soft landing, and together they were making it work on their own and discovering in the process a country of hidden beauty and cultural depth.

A couple of times they had returned to the land they'd bought in the region of Colon, between the Caribbean Sea and the Panama Canal. There he immediately set about establishing himself as an authority figure, someone to be reckoned with. The unofficial dumping of rubbish on his land was the first thing he attempted to tackle, sending a strongly worded letter in Anne's name to the village chief in Escobal, spelling out the benefits his company could bring to the local area – benefits that would be jeopardised if the illegal fly-tipping was allowed to continue.

For most of Anne's six-week holiday, however, the couple spent their time getting to know Panama City, and each other again. She was gradually realising that, like Diana before her, there had been a third person in her marriage over the past four years. The constant threat of discovery had hung between her and John like a theatrical blackout curtain, deadening their responses to each other and distorting all attempts at communication, but now that had lifted it was as if they were finally free to be themselves again – the selves they'd been before they became Mrs Widow and Mr Dead.

John was smiling again and making jokes. He'd started talking confidently and calmly about the future, rather than weighing in agitatedly with ever-changing, crazy schemes, or endlessly rehashing the past. Now he looked at people, rather than past them, and had even struck up a passing acquaintance with a couple of the neighbours in their apartment block.

When Anne had first booked her holiday, secretly she'd been a little anxious about she and John spending six weeks in each other's company. Many was the time when they were stuck together in the Seaton Carew house that she'd had to restrain herself from throwing open the door and simply running down the street, so strong was her desire to be free of him and his stifling presence. But the six weeks in Panama seemed to fly by as quickly as the toucans they'd seen in the forests – gone in a flap of wings and a blur of colour. And all too soon there was another leave-taking, another airport farewell.

Our Man in Panama

'It won't be for long,' John told her, noticing how pale she looked, despite the light tan. 'As soon as the house is sold you'll be out here again — for good this time.' She nodded, but inside she wasn't too reassured. She knew from experience how long it could take for a buyer to be found for her rambling home in Seaton Carew. Meanwhile she'd be living in limbo, half-moved out of one life but not quite ready for the next.

She hadn't been home long before she realised she'd been right to worry. Even though it was August, the month when Seaton Carew really came alive, somehow she felt distanced from it all. Normally she loved seeing the beach crammed with children, building sandcastles and squealing in the shallow water, their brightly coloured armbands bobbing jauntily as they jumped the gentle waves. She loved the noise people on holiday made, the sheer exuberant pleasure in voices that knew they didn't have to be measured or controlled or iron-fistedly diplomatic for a whole fortnight. And she loved how friendly the sea looked from her window when it was liberally dotted with rubber rings and lilos, inflatable dinghies and sailboards, like a much-cherished but garishly decorated Christmas tree.

But that summer of 2007 she just couldn't enter into the spirit of things as in previous years. She didn't spend hours looking out at the crowded sands, an indulgent smile playing around her mouth, perhaps remembering how she used to bring her own boys there when they were young, before they'd even imagined living in one of the imposing seaside villas.

Instead, when at home she paced the rooms, rather as John had done during those long years of his imprisonment. Unable to relax, she picked up newspapers only to put them down again minutes later, unread. The only things she could concentrate on were those tasks directly linked to her new life in Panama. She took to spending time in her study, poring over *Teach Yourself Spanish*, or on the Internet, reading up all she could about Panamanian history.

John's emails from Panama were bursting with descriptions of places he'd visited and information he'd found out. He'd regained that jocular, slightly boasting tone of old and was clearly in his element finding out the best way for them to disperse their money once it came through. Being back in financial control brought out the old seaside-postcard humour that up to 2002 he had revelled in. 'Get your bum over here fast,' he urged her. 'I've got something for you, and it's hot!'

Now Anne was openly telling people that she planned to move to Panama when the house was sold, explaining she'd fallen in love with the country and wanted to start life afresh – a completely blank canvas as it were. But if acquaintances were surprised, in the end they were generally accepting. 'Who can blame her?' they whispered, once she was out of earshot. 'This place must hold such terrible memories for her. Imagine seeing the place your husband died every time you look out the window.'

At work Anne's colleagues were glad to see her so full of plans, but slightly worried that the quiet, self-contained woman was taking such an uncharacteristic gamble. Was she thinking entirely straight? Would she one day regret it? Their concern increased when suddenly Anne seemed to be spending so much time on her mobile. Everybody took the occasional personal call at work, but she would talk away for ages, in hushed tones as if keen that no one should hear what she was saying. Perhaps there was a man on the scene in Panama, people wondered, but why the great secrecy?

One of her colleagues in particular grew suspicious of the furtive phone calls. There was something about them, the way she would hunch over her phone, turning her back to the rest of the room, that didn't seem quite right. The other woman started paying closer attention to what was being said, and she reached a most startling conclusion.

Anne Darwin was talking to her dead husband.

While her colleague was preparing to voice her suspicions to the police, Anne herself had a major breakthrough. The estate agent she'd contracted to sell her house rang to say there was someone interested in the property.

Like the Darwins before him, chemical process operator John Duffield had fallen in love with the location of No. 3 The Cliff. Looking around, he quickly realised it needed a lot of work, but also that it had tremendous potential. He felt rather sorry for Anne Darwin, the widow who'd been landed with the upkeep of the enormous property, and didn't blame her for wanting to get shot of it.

The price was £295,000 – a considerable sum in those parts, but not too bad for a property of that size and in that position.

'It's agreed!' the relieved estate agent told Mrs Darwin, thrilled to have some positive news at last. 'You're free!'

Five years before they'd faced defaulting on their mortgage and losing everything. Now a combination of rising property prices and John's faked death had netted them a fortune of half a million pounds. At last came the news that she had been waiting to hear for months. Finally she could start the mammoth task of packing up the house, stowing away in boxes mementoes of a past that now felt as if it belonged to another person altogether.

On John's instructions she set about applying for a police check so that her identity could be verified in anticipation of getting a Panamanian visa. Handing in her notice at work, she couldn't quite believe what she heard her own voice saying: that she was giving up her job, quitting the north-east, starting afresh on a completely different continent. Yes, she'd given it a lot of thought, she assured everyone. No, she wasn't rushing into anything.

Anthony and Mark were understandably anxious. They just couldn't imagine their mother setting up a life for herself on her own halfway across the world. But then she'd been so different recently, so positive-thinking and adventurous. Maybe, with John no longer on the scene, she was discovering a side of her personality that she'd never known before. They were proud of her independent spirit, and relieved she was taking control of her own destiny rather than sitting at home waiting to slide into unremarkable old age.

'Your mum's so brave,' friends would tell them admiringly. And they had to agree. Who'd have thought, when Dad disappeared in such terrible circumstances, that Mam would find the strength to turn her life around like this?

By October, as police tipped off by her suspicious colleague were starting to make their discreet enquiries, Anne had the house more or less packed up and ready to go. Of course, there were still bits of furniture lying around that she didn't want and various books and other things in the study, but there was a limit to what one woman could do on her own, and she felt she'd done her best.

Neighbours, seeing the respectable Mrs Darwin making journeys to and from her car with bin bags full of possessions, were surprised to be told she was leaving the country, although her exact destination seemed unclear. Jamaica, some thought, while others could have sworn she said Australia. It was a sudden decision, she told them, an impulse.

The weekend before she was due to leave for Panama, Mark and Anthony came to stay. It was a special time for all of them, with Anne veering between excitement at what she was going to and nostalgia for what she was leaving behind. Seeing her boys' anxious faces as they asked her again if she was sure she was doing the right thing, she so longed to tell them that they needn't be alarmed, that she wouldn't in fact be alone; she wanted to tell them all about how she and John would be starting again in the little fourth-storey flat, how different John was now, how dynamic. How they'd fallen in love for a second time, and exchanged emails saying how much they missed one another. She wished she could tell them about the resort they were planning to build, about the quality of the sunlight bouncing off the surface of Lake Gatún. But she couldn't do any of those things, so instead she reassured them as best she could, hoping to convey in the confidence of her manner all that she wasn't allowed to put into words.

'I really am fine,' she told them. 'I'm so excited to be going.'

To prove how she'd done her research she told them that the proceeds from the sale of the house would go into a company, in which the boys were named as shareholders. There was a complicated explanation as to why this worked best. Naturally her sons weren't about to be obstructive.

Saying goodbye to the boys was hard, but she kept telling them that it wasn't for long. Why had she bought a two-bedroom flat, if not in the expectation of constant visitors, she warned them? Anyway, after 90 days she'd need to get a tourist visa in order to stay in Panama and she might well be coming back to the UK to sort it out. They wouldn't be rid of her so easily.

Emotions were running high that weekend, as a bitter Mark and Anthony would later recall in an interview with a Sunday newspaper, and at no point more so than when Anne told her sons: 'I want you to have some of Dad's things.' Mark and Anthony were choked. Anne had been so loath for any of John's possessions to leave the house after he'd died, despite their gentle nudges. 'I still miss your father every single day,' she continued, her soft voice wavering. 'But now I'm leaving the house and the life we had here, it's time to let go of some of those memories.'

She asked the boys to choose some keepsakes from among John's personal possessions. Biting back the tears, they sifted carefully through the things Anne hadn't been able to bring herself to get rid of. Mark selected his father's black onyx cufflinks and his watch, while Anthony chose his wedding ring, passport and an old pocket watch. He also picked out a few of his dad's books from the shelf. It wasn't until much later, when the truth about John's disappearance had come out, that he'd look at these more carefully and realise one of the books was dated 2003 – the year *after* John had gone missing.

Once the boys had gone, suddenly the house felt very quiet and empty, the deadened silence almost a reproach. Anne felt like a fugitive fleeing the scene of a crime, a rat deserting the proverbial sinking ship. The house's denuded walls, with their blotchy darker patches where pictures had once hung, seemed to accuse her of something. Neglect? Insufficient care? Dust stirred up by the moving of furniture left untouched for years hung in the air in front of the windows as if suspended in time.

She wandered from room to room, desultorily picking up the few remaining possessions and randomly cramming them into boxes and bags, or just putting them back down again. None of this seemed real, this process of shedding the detritus of one life ready to be reborn into another. She felt as if she were a ghost, haunting her own self as she moved aimlessly about the house waiting for the removal van to arrive.

The end when it came was, as these things inevitably are, an anticlimax. After the drama of their years in Seaton Carew, the 'accident' at sea, the reunion, the years in hiding, Anne Darwin slipped away with barely a trace on 17 October 2007. Passing through empty, abandoned rooms, down the echoing hallway, her footsteps padding soundlessly on threadbare carpets, she opened the same front door through which her gaunt, dishevelled husband had entered four years before when he'd come back from the dead. Then, without drama or backward glance, she slipped outside, pulling the heavy door shut behind her and entombing within the house, with a single, final click, the secrets of the past five years.

Was it just fancy, or did she really feel lighter as she turned her back on No. 3 and walked away for the last time, each step putting more distance between herself and a life that already felt like someone else's?

Settling in behind the wheel of the car, she paused for just a moment to adjust her glasses, but even then she was careful to keep her eyes fixed straight ahead on the removal van in front of her. And then she was off, dropping off the keys to the house with the estate agent, before disappearing from the locality for good, slipping off the radar with as little fuss as a leaf falling from a tree.

Arrangements had been made for the furniture to be shipped off to its new home in Panama. The removal company estimated it should be there in around six weeks. By that time, she hoped – as she watched the van pull off with its cargo of furniture and keepsakes, the leftovers of their life – she and John would be comfortably settled into their new home and Hartlepool would seem a distant memory, a word written on an airline address label.

As her plane took off, the urban sprawl of Newcastle growing ever smaller in the distance, she had the strangest sensation of stepping out of herself, as if, snake-like, she were shedding her skin in readiness for becoming someone else. The north-east, England, all that was behind her now. Ahead was only the clear blue sky of an endless, limitless world.

Racing headlong into her brave new world, flight socks firmly on feet, she could have no idea that before the furniture had even turned up on her newly scrubbed Panamanian doorstep, she'd be flying back to the UK, her tropical dream in tatters, and accompanied by a brace of armed policemen.

11
LIVING THE DREAM

All through the long flight to Panama City Anne imagined how her new life would unfurl before her like a red carpet once she arrived in her adopted home country. After the successful holiday with John in July she was looking forward to seeing him again with an almost girlish intensity. Now the nightmare of the past few years was behind them they could finally get to know each other all over again, establishing new ground rules for a relationship that would necessarily be completely different.

But after only a few hours on Panamanian soil she started to realise that things might not turn out just as she'd hoped. Now the house was sold and there was so much money hanging about, the problem was that John had become fixated on making sure they were getting the best possible return for their savings and, more importantly, that there was no way the cash could be traced from the UK. After various fees had been paid out Anne was left with about

£280,000 from the sale of the second Seaton Carew house. Although the house had been in the boys' names the proceeds had been wired on to Panama and were sitting in the bank account that she had opened there when they bought the land and the apartment.

But John wasn't happy. 'We're not earning enough interest that way,' he insisted. 'I've been round all the different banks finding out which pay the best rates. Plus, I think we should open several different accounts so it's much harder to trace and we don't attract so much suspicion.'

As the accounts had to be in Anne's name, what he actually meant was that he thought she should open a few accounts. She wasn't convinced and she felt that already she'd done her bit – she'd sold the house in England and now she was exhausted. She just wanted to relax for a bit with John, pottering about the apartment or the city. The last thing she wanted was to become drawn into a whole lot more paperwork, with all the anxieties that involved. From opening just one bank account she knew the procedure wasn't so straightforward as it sounded. Surely they had enough money? They wouldn't miss a few dollars here and there.

But he was adamant. For weeks he'd been trailing around the city researching the best financial deals. This was what it had all been leading to – all their patience, all his planning, and he was determined to squeeze every last cent of interest out of the money they had. Reluctantly she accompanied her husband on a tour of the city's financial institutions, with John growing increasingly frustrated.

'Why didn't you ask them what I told you?' he'd say, exasperated, as they exited yet another glass-fronted bank.

Living the Dream

'I just forgot,' she would answer, cross and flustered. 'I still don't understand why we have to do this.'

He would storm ahead, fuming. It infuriated him that Anne was the one with her name on the bank accounts — it left him feeling powerless and, well, exposed. After all his hard work sometimes he felt like he still had no control over his life, and this was hard to accept. It would be different when they had the hotel up and running, he told himself; then they'd be equal partners.

Anne was also having her doubts. She hated going into a bank and queuing up to see some intimidating official, her hands clammy with nerves, her mind going over and over what John had instructed her to say. She'd just left everything behind to start a new life in the sun and all they seemed to be doing was waiting in endless queues, filling in forms and arguing.

'I just want to make sure we're set up, what's wrong with that?' John would demand.

'What about what *I* want?' Anne would snap. 'Sometimes I think I'd have been better off staying at home.'

It was not, she reflected as they stood stonily side by side in the apartment block's compact lift, both staring fixedly ahead, the way she'd envisaged the first fortnight of their new life. Still less could she have predicted that all these boring, petty financial details would have to be later relived in front of a packed courtroom.

There was also the visa problem. While John had been in Panama he'd learned that there were to be changes to the country's visa requirements. If they wanted to stay there indefinitely they'd need an investor's visa, which would then involve getting their identities checked and verified by the British police. Of course no problem for Anne with her squeaky-clean past, but a huge setback for a supposedly vanished man, travelling on a passport in the name of a baby who'd been dead since 1950.

The only way around it, as far as John could see, was to do exactly what he'd spent the past five and a half years avoiding – to reveal himself as John Darwin. On a meticulously drawn-up spreadsheet which Sky News found among emails sent between the couple and that made Anne's head spin just to look at, he plotted out their options to her, with the best-case and worst-case scenarios highlighted in different colours.

'I'll go back and pretend to have amnesia,' he told her. 'You know me – I'm a good actor when I want to be. They might think it's odd, but they'll never be able to prove anything. Then I'll apply for a passport and driving licence in my real name and come straight back. No one has seen me in the last five years. There's nothing to show I'm lying. What's the worst thing that could happen?'

He was convinced Panama was far enough from the UK to make it impossible to trace their money. 'I'd be long gone by the time they started trying to recover any insurance money,' he explained to Anne. 'And even if they did try to get some back, or, God forbid, all the initial £250,000 insurance payout, we'd still have a quarter of a million left from the house sales.'

'You're crazy,' she told him when she realised he was serious. 'All those years in England and you stayed hidden away, and now we're finally able to start living the life we'd planned, you want to go back and turn yourself in.' But he couldn't see an alternative. He wanted to be able to stay indefinitely in Panama without fear of falling foul of the authorities. Besides, there was so much more to be gained from becoming John Darwin again – his sons, for a start.

The amnesia story would mean that he could legitimately get in touch with Mark and Anthony again. Just the thought of giving them a hug, or going out cycling with them, even picking up the phone for a chat, made him almost giddy with excitement. For five and a half years he hadn't allowed himself to think about spending time with his boys, but now that he'd started to entertain the possibility of being back in their lives he found he couldn't bear to consider any alternative. If he now imagined staying in Panama and never going back to being John Darwin, father of two, he felt the loss of his boys more keenly than ever before.

And why shouldn't this work? People suffered amnesia all the time after a blow to the head. His kayak could have been hit by a boat, for instance. Sometimes they didn't discover their true identity for months, even years. Why would anyone suspect him of anything? All the money was out of the UK now and it would be very complicated for the authorities to try to reclaim it, particularly now that they, or at least Anne, had bought property in Panama.

Just thinking about the property made the plan even more attractive. As it stood, there was nothing to show that he had rights over the flat or the land itself. What if they built up a successful business and then had a blazing row and Anne cut him off without a cent? The way things were at the moment he was 100 per cent dependent on her charity and that was, to his way of thinking, a very unhealthy state of affairs.

If nothing changed he could find himself on the streets of Panama with nothing. Whereas if John Darwin turned out miraculously not to be dead after all, he'd be able to have bank accounts in his name and property deeds; he would get back his sons and his financial autonomy. It was risky, but the rewards would be staggering.

Ever the pedant, John started to research amnesia. The kind of amnesia he'd be more likely to have had – long-term post-traumatic – was most often caused by a blow to the head, which would certainly be consistent with his kayak being hit by a boat. Last September's news was dominated by *Top Gear* presenter Richard Hammond, who suffered short-term post-traumatic amnesia after damaging his brain during a high-speed car crash. For John the only trouble was that the kind of amnesia that lasts years is very rare and would almost invariably be accompanied by severe physical and mental disabilities. Would anyone be taken in?

He realised that it would be impossible for him to claim that he had been in a coma all that time. Medical records would need to be produced and the truth would soon come out, but what if he just said that he couldn't remember anything at all from before the accident? How could anyone possibly prove differently?

'Just put it out of your head,' Anne told him repeatedly. She was firmly of the mind that dead people really ought to stay dead and that it was tempting fate for them to start popping up years later, pretending not to know who they were. But then she also knew how stubborn John could be.

'Just think, it'd all be out in the open,' he explained persuasively.

Living the Dream

'The boys could come over to see us, even move over here if they wanted to. We'd be a family again.'

Sinking back into her padded garden chair, she felt a sense of weary resignation begin to settle over her, heavy as the Panama heat, as she listened to John growing ever more enthusiastic about his plan. 'Nobody will really be that bothered about me,' he decided. 'Thousands of people go missing every year and then turn up again. I'd just be another one of them.'

Seeing the unconvinced expression on his wife's face, he tried to win her over. 'Five years ago we had nothing but debt and now look at us,' he said, waving a hand around at the blue sky and the gently rustling palm tree. 'You didn't believe I could do it, but I did. You've just got to have a bit of faith.'

Had he added the phrase 'When have I ever let you down?', as for one horrible moment it seemed he might, Anne might have lost her temper, but thankfully he kept his counsel. However, the look on his face spoke volumes – it was an expression that she'd seen so many times before and she knew exactly what it meant: 'I'm one step ahead of them. I can beat the system.'

But bureaucracy wasn't the only thing causing John to lie awake at night on their brand-new double mattress, his skin like treacle in the sticky heat. Since Anne had rejoined him in Panama all they seemed to do was argue, and he was starting to wonder if there might not be a darker reason behind their growing estrangement. What if she had started seeing someone else?

The idea wasn't too far-fetched – after all, he himself had had his Internet flirtations and had even gone out to stay with Kelly

Steele. What if she had met someone else while they'd been apart and was even now planning to bring him over to Panama to be part of her exciting shiny new future? Glancing over at his wife, he had to tell himself to stop being so ridiculous. She looked exactly the same as ever, with her undyed hair and her comfortable if rather shapeless clothes. If she was carrying hidden secrets they were well disguised indeed. And yet, once the idea came into his head, he just couldn't seem to shake it free.

The truth was, he realised with growing unease, if Anne did want to take up with someone else it would leave him, well, permanently marooned up shit creek without a paddle. He had no rights to the properties they'd bought, or indeed to the money stashed away in bank accounts: he was a dead man, with a made-up passport. He had no past, and without her, no future either. He'd arrived at 57 years of age to find himself totally dependent on someone else and it wasn't a good feeling.

While they were out traipsing around banks he'd watch Anne with an expression not altogether dissimilar to the one he'd worn as a prison officer in Holme House – wariness combined with thoughtfulness and a smile that never went any deeper than the surface, as though stuck on with glue. It wasn't so much the thought of her with someone else that upset him – after the wilderness years following his disappearance he'd had to consider that possibility before – it was the knowledge of his own helplessness. Every time she frowned or retreated behind her book, or snapped at him in yet another bank queue, he was struck anew by the sickening realisation that everything he'd risked, everything he'd suffered, could all be for nothing. If she wanted to she could disinherit him on a whim, leaving him penniless in Panama. Another man could help her spend her widow's pension and design the perfect hotel at Lake Gatún; he could reap all the benefits of his sacrifices and there would be nothing he could do about it.

Anne couldn't help noticing how withdrawn John had become of late, but rather than try to jolly him out of it, as she would probably have done another time, she decided to let him stew. After all, it was his fault things were going so badly. Why didn't he realise that after overseeing the sale of the house and all the packing up, she was completely exhausted and all she wanted to do was to take it easy and unwind in their new flat? Any man with an ounce of sensitivity would have understood how much it had taken out of her to handle the move and say goodbye to the boys. He should have been bringing her cups of tea in bed, rather than insisting she get up early so they could trudge around the city filling in dull but scary-looking forms.

Every now and then she'd catch him gazing over at her with a strange, questioning expression on his face as if she were one of the mathematical problems he used to set his class during his teaching days. She knew he was anxious about something. Well, good, let him fret! Maybe then he'd have some idea about the pressure she'd been under over the past couple of months.

After the fantastic holiday they'd shared just a few short months before, both of them had had high expectations of their reunion in Panama and were more than a little dismayed to find that the early friction between them showed no signs of easing up. In fact they found they were increasingly getting on each other's nerves. Anne hated the seemingly endless trips to banks and building societies, the filling in of forms, the signing of cheques – all the time with that slight edge of panic hovering in the back of her mind that she might say something to give the game away or reveal some glaring inconsistency in her story.

John, for his part, was incensed that he couldn't just take care of all the paperwork himself. It infuriated him to have to follow Anne around from place to place like a lapdog when he was so much more capable of taking charge of it all. He felt embittered that it was his sacrifice that had earned them all this money, yet it was Anne who controlled it.

After a couple of weeks of bickering and sniping she finally reached breaking point. 'I wish we'd never come to Panama,' she sobbed, looking out from the balcony at the view that had once given her such a thrill but now seemed only to intensify her feelings of being somewhere alien and far from home.

John, who'd been thinking more or less the same, now came up with another of his impulse plans. What they needed to do, he decided, was get away from Panama City for a bit, maybe explore around a little, spend more time together and remind themselves why they'd come.

He and Anne were becoming so estranged and if he didn't get her back on board with the whole scheme everything would be lost. 'Let's go on holiday,' he suggested.

A few weeks before it would have seemed inconceivable to Anne that they could be sitting in the sunshine, with the Pacific ocean glittering in the distance, and be talking seriously about needing a 'holiday'. But she knew that if they didn't take a break there was a good chance they'd end up hating either each other or their new adopted homeland, even both. After much discussion they decided to go to Costa Rica for a week. It says a lot about how far they'd come in the past few years that they talked about exploring Central America with the same level of dispassionate interest as, years before, they might have discussed a caravanning holiday in Scotland.

Bordering on Panama, Costa Rica wasn't a major expedition and as, like Panama, British nationals could stay without a visa for up to three months, travelling there wouldn't be a problem. They could even drive there in the US$41,000 Toyota Land Cruiser John had insisted on buying. But it was somewhere different, a place they could relax together away from the pressures of Panama.

So, in the middle of November, with the Panamanian sun still lazily limbering up in readiness for the summer season, the Darwins heaved their bags into the lift of their apartment block, loaded up the boot of their luxury car and set off. Their destination was the Costa Rican resort of Cahuita, a beautiful yet peaceful beach community on the Atlantic coast, around 60 kilometres from the Panamanian border. There, against the backdrop of the stunning national park with its rainforests and rapids, edged by mile upon mile of deserted sandy beach, they slowly began to unwind.

As they sat by the hotel pool the tensions of the past fortnight faded away like sunscreen on skin. For a few precious days they didn't talk about the future, or about John's madcap scheme to reclaim his place among the living. Instead they just lay on loungers reading books or took long walks along the beaches, where palm trees leaned out over the sand as if reaching for the sea and horses galloped effortlessly past, the muffled thud of their hooves hanging in the humid air well after they'd disappeared from view.

In the evenings they'd eat seafood fresh from the fishing boats or, if they were feeling adventurous, some of the local Caribbean dishes, such as rice and beans, or fish in coconut sauce. Over dinner they'd talk languorously about things they'd seen that day, or what they might do the next – deliberately not looking further ahead than the next swim, the next sunset.

A couple of times they rode horses along the beach. After the sustained nightmare of the past five years, for Anne it was sheer exhilaration to feel the warm breeze on her face as the scenery whirled past in a blur of vivid greens and blues. Watching her up ahead, her white hair tucked out of sight under a baseball cap, a broad smile lighting up her face, John wondered at how young she suddenly looked, once again the girl from the sweetshop he'd tried so hard to impress.

They could have stayed in Cahuita indefinitely, putting on hold their troubled history and their uncertain future, but one morning, while checking her emails on the hotel computer, Anne found a message from the removal company saying her furniture would be arriving in Panama on 7 December – three weeks earlier than she'd previously thought. 'But they won't let the stuff into the country unless I can prove I've applied for a visa!' she wailed. And applying for a visa meant yet more paperwork. There was no way around it – they'd have to head back to Panama.

The last night in Cahuita finally they talked about the things they'd been avoiding all week.

Living the Dream

'I can't stop thinking about going back to England,' John told Anne, his voice soft and curiously disembodied in the Costa Rican darkness. 'I really think the amnesia thing will work. When do you think the best time would be for me to go?'

She gazed at him while a mixture of incredulity, frustration and sheer exasperation seized hold of her. 'John, there will *never* be a good time to go!' she eventually told him. 'Can't you understand that?'

He nodded, but she could tell that he thought he knew better. There was a familiar set to his mouth, a sudden wariness in his eyes as if he were holding something back.

'Fine,' he told her, his voice already changed – tighter, lower and as if weighted down with secrets. 'It's your choice. If you don't want me to go I won't.'

Even as he said it she realised it wasn't a choice at all but an already secure outcome that would lie fully formed on the ground between them until it was finally allowed to come to life. It was always the way with John – once he'd made up his mind about something he was never quite able to let it go, but carried it around with him like a tin can tied to a dog's tail.

All through the journey back to Panama City his plan sat wedged between them like an extra passenger. Anne tried to talk around it, but always there was the awareness that some obstacle was in the way, something that needed to be dislodged. Eventually, not long after they'd got back to their apartment, she gave in to what had, all along, been inevitable: 'All right! If this is something you really feel you have to do, go ahead. I'd rather you did it now and got it over with. We won't ever be able to get on with our lives with it hanging over our heads.'

Up The Creek Without a Paddle

On the Internet she found him a flight back to the UK, her fingers wavering momentarily before clicking on the 'return' option. And then it was booked. Friday, 30 November 2007: the date John Darwin would set off to find himself again.

'But what will you say?' Anne must have asked him the same question a hundred times in the days leading up to his departure, yet she still wasn't satisfied by any of his responses.

'I'll just say I don't remember,' he told her yet again. 'I'll tell people I can't remember anything past that holiday in Norway we took.'

For some reason he latched on to the family break they'd had in Norway in 2000 as his point of no return. He would claim not to remember anything about buying the houses in Seaton Carew, the mounting debt, or the day he paddled out to sea in a red kayak and didn't come home again; he wouldn't remember turning back up again, or the years spent in hiding or indeed the Panama experience.

He'd announce that he'd only just remembered who he was, his date of birth and that he thought he was missing, and that he had no memory of the past seven years. Of course there'd be some questions, scratching of heads perhaps, maybe a few warnings about having to repay any life insurance, but then he'd be reunited with his boys and officially with Anne, and the second phase of his life could begin.

Anne didn't mention that his story had a hole in it bigger than the one in his mangled kayak. Instead she pointed out the more glaring discrepancies in the tale, such as how to explain away his Panamanian tan.

Living the Dream

'It'll be fine,' he told her vaguely. 'In fact it'll work to my advantage. I don't want it to look like I've been locked away inside for the past few years.'

But when she asked what impression he did want to give, he was noncommittal.

'Don't worry so much,' he told her. 'I've got a good feeling about this – everything will be OK.'

Even so, when the day for his departure dawned he was feeling a good deal less cocky than he tried to appear. It was one thing to talk about giving himself up, but another thing entirely to imagine actually doing it. What would he do? Turn up at a hospital, at his brother's house in London or at the old place in Seaton Carew?

How does a man in the grip of amnesia comport himself? Does he stagger in, clutching his head in his hands, like in the movies? Or would he stride purposefully up to an authority figure in a direct, no-nonsense kind of way?

Gathering his things ready to leave, he was overwhelmed by a mixture of excitement and dread, which he tried unsuccessfully to keep at bay by focusing on how it would be when he returned to Panama, once again a living, breathing man with an identity and a past plus a future – most of all, with a right to pick up the phone and call his sons, or to argue with his wife without fear of being left destitute.

As they waited for the taxi that would take him to the airport the atmosphere throbbed with emotional charge. Both of them were consumed by doubts and fears, though for slightly different reasons. In addition to her worries about John, Anne was dreading

185

being left behind in Panama to cope alone with overseeing the arrival of their furniture and all the continuing red tape about visas and bank accounts. It was one thing being on extended holiday there, in the constant company of her husband, but another thing entirely to be stuck there on her own, trying to manage complicated arrangements, with only the most basic grasp of Spanish.

Meanwhile John was still dithering over all the differing versions of the story that he was going to tell when he got back to the UK. Every few minutes he'd decide on a definitive line, only to change it again a short while later after trying it out in his mind. He was still confident it would work, but suddenly it felt such a huge step and he wished Anne was going with him. Still in the back of his mind was the kernel of suspicion that maybe she did have a man hidden away somewhere, ready to slip into his shoes as soon as he was gone.

Their goodbye was uncharacteristically intense, each holding on to the other as though clutching at a dream that seemed to be slipping through their fingers like sand on Cahuita beach.

'Don't worry, Anne,' he told her again, finally pulling away and picking up his case. 'The next time you see me everything will be completely different.'

As he walked away with a slight wave of his hand neither of them had any idea that for once, in this respect at least, John Darwin would turn out to be absolutely right.

12
'I THINK I MIGHT BE MISSING!'

West End Central police station, at 27 Savile Row in London's Mayfair, is an unprepossessing building, made of grey stone blocks and blending in with neighbouring offices on the street famous for its elite men's tailoring. According to local legend its name was changed from the Savile Row police station because the smartest tailoring firms considered that it somehow tarnished their reputation to have the street's illustrious name linked to premises where crooks and other dubious characters congregated.

Owing to its central, upmarket location, over the years the station has seen a parade of the famous and infamous climb the wide steps leading up to the main entrance. The previous year newspaper front pages had featured shots of Jamiroquai singer Jay Kay being bundled up to the front desk after allegedly assaulting a photographer outside a nearby nightclub. But the middle-aged man who made his way up the steps at 5.30pm on Saturday, 1 December 2007 was not anyone you'd recognise – not yet anyway.

Looking fit and tanned but otherwise unremarkable, he walked determinedly towards the front desk. From his clothes and general demeanour anyone watching would have guessed that he had come in to report a stolen bag, or perhaps to ask directions. And so it was a surprise when, after clearing his throat, the rather nondescript man announced: 'I think I'm a missing person.'

At their respective homes in London and Hampshire, Mark and Anthony Darwin were halfway through what appeared to be a typical early December weekend. Anthony, 29, was with wife of two years, Louise, at their home in Basingstoke, while 31-year-old Mark was enjoying being a guest at a wedding in south London. He'd just moved into a shared house in Finchley which he'd found through an ad, so it felt good to unwind in the company of good friends and his girlfriend Felicia Witts, known to everyone as 'Flick'.

Both brothers were still feeling rather shell-shocked at their mother's sudden decision to uproot to Central America, but were gradually coming to terms with the idea of having a long-distance parent and had been talking about making their first trip out to Panama to see her. Meanwhile their own lives continued much the same as before. Anthony had resigned from his job as an insurance broker with Towergate Risk Solutions in Reading in August of that year and was still trying to decide which career path to follow next. Mark, by bizarre coincidence – which some doubters would later and completely misguidedly deem highly suspicious – had also quit his job, as a software developer at international property consultancy EC Harris, just the previous day and was savouring his first day of leisure.

And so both Darwin boys were in a chilled-out, reflective mood that first weekend in December 2007, but the anonymous tranquillity of their lives was about to be irrevocably shattered.

'There's somebody here who says he's your dad.'

The woman on the other end of the phone sounded slightly hesitant, as if she wasn't quite sure how the news she had to break would go down. She said she was from Hartlepool police and that a man claiming to be John Darwin had turned up at a police station in London. For a moment, as Mark would later describe in a detailed interview with a newspaper following his mother's trial, he wasn't sure he'd heard properly through the din of the wedding reception.

His *dad*?

How many times had he and his brother dreamed of hearing those words, yet now they didn't seem real, just a selection of random sounds that made no sense at all. For five years the Darwin boys had searched for an answer to the riddle of their father's disappearance, following up reports on missing people who'd turned up unexpectedly, chasing all leads on unidentified bodies. And somewhere, over the years, they'd managed to come to terms with the idea that they might never unravel the truth of what happened, that it really was possible to paddle out to sea on a perfectly still spring day and never be heard of again.

And now they were being told that their father had strolled into a London police station, just as calmly as if he were returning from a quick trip to the supermarket. He apparently had no memory of the past seven years and had been spotted wandering in Topshop, muttering about his wife and his dogs. Once he'd been guided to West Central station he'd managed to piece together some few crucial details such as his name and birth date. A quick Google on the Internet ascertained that John Darwin was indeed a missing person and the subject of an ongoing inquiry by Cleveland police — whose operational area includes Hartlepool — and that is how they'd got in touch with his sons.

At first Mark was stunned, but then he felt angry. It couldn't be his dad after all these years, he decided; it would turn out to be a hoax. And yet in the back of his mind was a tiny spark of hope that grew bigger with every passing second. Why would anyone pretend to be his dad? Wasn't it just possible that he really could turn up after all this time? He stood rooted to the spot and everything went into slow motion as he considered the idea that his dad really could be back from the dead.

As Mark and Flick made their way by tube to the police station, by turns ecstatic and apprehensive, Anthony and Louise were being informed of John's reappearance at their home in Basingstoke. Again there was the same mixture of shock, incredulity and excitement as they jumped in the car ready to head into central London. In fact Anthony was in such a state that he got completely lost and needed a police escort to the station.

Neither of them knew what to expect. Unlike their father, who'd had five and a half years to think about this reunion, Mark and Anthony came to it utterly unprepared. Though it had taken a long time for them to give up all hope after his disappearance, they'd eventually had to accept that he was dead. For five years they'd tried to come to terms with the fact, each suffering bouts of black depression. And now they were being told he wasn't dead after all. It just didn't make sense.

The brothers would wait until after their parents' fate was revealed in court to go public with how they'd been reunited with their father. As he'd tell the newspaper which first ran the interview, Mark was first on the scene. As he made his way into the station, gripping Flick's hand tightly, he felt as if each breath was being torn painfully out of him. Who would he find when he entered the building? Could it really be his father, or would it turn out to be an impostor, a sad stranger who'd assumed his name?

He was shown into a small room, where a police officer produced three photographs of the man claiming to be John Darwin. Mark instantly recognised him.

'That's *him*!' he exclaimed in disbelief. 'That's my dad!'

He was still shaking when the policeman announced gently: 'I'm going to bring him in now.'

Part of Mark still refused to believe that he was about to be reunited with the father he'd presumed dead for the last five years. But the man who was led in to meet him a few minutes later was no stranger. He was much thinner, and somehow smaller, with less hair and a pronounced tan, but he was undeniably, irrefutably, his dad.

Mark would later tell the newspaper that it felt like everything in the world stopped at that moment, as he and his father gazed at each other.

'I didn't believe it was you,' he said eventually.

John appeared calm but exhausted. 'Where's your Mam?' he asked. 'And the dogs?' As if in a spell, Mark told him the dogs had died and John seemed resigned. 'They were good, loyal dogs,' he said.

Then he wanted to know who Flick was, and as the introductions were made, they all hugged, and Mark could feel the tears burning in his eyes. 'I missed you,' he sobbed.

A police psychologist had warned him John was very fragile and that he shouldn't press him about where he'd been, so Mark bit back the questions that rushed through his mind. Instead he focused on the one sure-fire certainty: his father was alive and well.

When Anthony arrived the scene was repeated again. For a full ten minutes after John greeted him with a hug, his younger son gazed at him without speaking a word, just drinking him in with his eyes. It didn't seem possible. His father, dead for these last five and a half years, was now sitting in front of him.

The Darwin boys were told they could take John home with them that night, but anxious to ensure Anne didn't hear the news from anyone else before they had a chance to tell her themselves, they decided to call her from the police station.

Still trembling, Mark dialled his mother's still unfamiliar number. Right up until she answered the phone he had no idea what he was going to say to her. How do you break it to a woman who's been a widow for more than five years that her husband is still alive?

'I Think I Might Be Missing!'

It was evening when the phone sounded in Anne Darwin's Panama City apartment, five hours behind Greenwich Mean Time.

'Hello, Mam, is that you?'

Her heart lurched painfully as she registered the excitement in her son's voice.

This is it, she thought to herself. There's no going back now.

'Is everything OK?' she asked, almost on autopilot.

Mark's words came tumbling out, light and fast as bubbles from one of the bubble guns he'd played with as a child.

'Mam, brace yourself. I've got something to tell you. Are you sitting down? You'll never believe it, Mam. I'm sitting here with Dad!'

Anne, who'd been steeling herself for this moment ever since waving John off at Panama City Airport, had worried about whether she'd be able to fake emotion, but in the event hearing the sheer happiness and exhilaration in her son's voice brought such a lump to her throat that she didn't have to pretend.

'Did I hear you right?' she murmured, her voice thick with sudden tears.

'Yes, Mam,' came the jubilant response. 'Dad is home!'

She didn't have time to think, only to react to the sheer amazement in her son's voice.

'Is he OK?' she asked faintly.

'Yes, he's absolutely fine.'

Before she knew what was going on a police officer came on the phone explaining how her husband had walked into the station, suffering from amnesia, without any recollection of the past seven years. And then suddenly the phone was being passed over to

193

someone else. There was an abrupt silence at the other end, followed by a familiar voice.

'Anne? Is that *really* you? Are you all right?'

And now for the first time, talking to the husband she'd said goodbye to only the day before, she really did have to act. But her voice echoed round the empty apartment, stilted and unconvincing.

'Yes, it's me,' she replied awkwardly. 'How are you?'

There followed a brief, equally strained exchange, but thankfully it was truncated by the boys' desperation to catch up with their long-lost father.

'I'll talk to you all soon,' Anne said uselessly, just before the receiver was put down at the other end. And then she was alone, thoughts churning inside her head like cement in a mixer. 'This is it,' she repeated to herself. 'It's really happened. No going back.'

The night before she'd sent John a chatty email, knowing he was still in transit. 'Don't leave me,' she'd written at the end, partly because that phrase had become a standing joke between them, and partly because she did indeed feel as if she was being abandoned. Now, knowing he'd set his mad plan into action, she was overcome by the same conflicting emotions.

Part of her was terrified. Now everything was all at stake she realised just how much there was to lose: the new life in Panama, her relationship with John, the loyalty of her sons... All of it could be gone in the space of time that it takes to make a phone call. But above the fear floated another sensation – weightless, irrepressible, her caution and dread drifted away like balloons.

Relief?

'I Think I Might Be Missing!'

Whatever happened now, it was all over. One way or another things would be different. There'd be no more lies, no more hiding. She wouldn't spend her whole life looking over her shoulder to see who was coming. Whatever happened now would happen. There'd be no more plans that changed as often as the weather, no agonising decisions to keep her awake through the muggy Panamanian night. All she had to do now was wait.

Meanwhile, back in the UK, John Darwin couldn't help but think that things were going exceptionally well. After he'd been grilled by the London police, first acting on their own and later with the help of their colleagues in Cleveland, he'd been released into the care of his sons, both of whom seemed so endearingly happy to see him that they hardly let him out of their sight.

Going back to Anthony's home with his two sons was such an exquisite pleasure. To finally be able to talk to them, to see them laugh, to study their faces in depth and marvel at how they'd matured over the last five years, seemed the most extraordinary privilege. And though he knew the police would want to talk to him again, trying to wheedle out any information about where he'd spent the past five years, he really felt it had gone pretty well so far. It was obvious they had far bigger fish to fry than a back-from-the-dead kayaker. He reckoned there'd be a bit of a stir about it, but when they realised he couldn't, or wouldn't, answer any questions about where he'd been, they'd soon get bored and move on. And in the meantime he'd get to spend some quality time with his sons at last.

By Sunday, 2 December the future according to John Darwin

was looking pretty rosy indeed. It was such a thrill to wake up in the same house as his boys, to be able to speak directly to them rather than listening to their voices through the wall or loudspeaker. Even more exciting was waking up with the knowledge that once again he existed. He had a place in the world, a right to be there, a name to claim as his own.

He was John Darwin, father of two, husband of Anne. He'd been lost for five years, but now he was home.

Later that day Mark and Anthony took him to Asda to buy him some clothes. All he had was the maroon zip-up sweatshirt and baggy beige trousers that he'd turned up in at the police station, together with what he'd been carrying in his pockets – cash and keys. Seeing Anthony's panic after he'd wandered off on his own, John jokingly reassured him: 'Don't worry, I'm not going to run off!'

But for the Darwin boys, deprived of their father for all those years, this was no laughing matter.

To John's dismay several newspapers on Monday morning featured reports of his 'miracle' reappearance. He'd hoped not to make too much of a splash but journalists seemed to be won over by the Back From the Dead Canoeist story (he was to discover over the next few weeks and months that 'canoeist' was deemed to have more descriptive power than 'kayaker', and once he'd been branded a canoeist this would prove an impossible label to shift). More worrying, several of the reports were written in an arch tone that seemed to imply a certain amount of cynicism about his amnesia account. John started to feel vaguely apprehensive as he read articles which included old quotes of Anne's saying how he couldn't have 'stage-managed' his disappearance.

Why were they digging all that up?

His concern increased when he saw that the papers were asking readers if anyone had any information about where he'd been for the past five years and that they were giving out details of a special hotline. Still, he refused to let worry spoil his reunion with his sons. It would all blow over soon, he told himself. So long as he stuck to his story about not being able to remember anything, he'd be OK. The papers would soon tire of the lack of any new information and it wasn't as if they'd been flooded with sightings of him over the past few years. He'd been so careful to disguise himself. All those years of staying inside, avoiding being seen would pay off, he was sure of it.

To add extra credence to his story he was careful to keep up the amnesia pretence, even at Anthony's house, as Anthony's wife would later recall in a newspaper report.

'What's this?' John asked innocently, when Louise served him fish for tea.

'I've never had fish,' he told them dreamily after he'd listened to her reply.

For those first magical few days he was blissfully happy spending time with his sons and finding out about their lives. Funny how, when you get older, five years can pass without anything of substance really altering, but one's twenties remain a time of massive changes – people fall in love, get married, start careers and suddenly switch them. There was so much to catch up on.

The following day John had another interview with the police already lined up, but he wasn't unduly panicked. After all, what could they really do? As long as he stuck to his story about not remembering anything since 2000 there was no way anyone could prove he was lying.

But by Tuesday, 4 December interest in the Back From the Dead Canoeist seemed to have increased, not waned. Journalists had managed to dig up facts about the day that he disappeared being calm, with a sea like glass. They'd talked to neighbours and discovered that his wife had moved abroad very suddenly, just a few weeks before. Also they'd tracked down his delighted father, who wondered whether a blow on the head sustained by John as a child might have contributed to his long-term amnesia. They'd also talked to an elderly aunt, who viewed his return to life with suspicion, adding damningly that there was some doubt he'd ever even got his feet wet.

Most damagingly, they'd managed to uncover evidence that someone using his name had applied for a credit card from the Seaton Carew address the year before. And each report was heavy with the weight of revelations about the level of debt the Darwins were in before John's mysterious disappearance, and how much money Anne might have stood to gain from his death. Yet still he refused to believe the game was up. Sure, there was innuendo and fingers were being pointed, but he'd get past all that. He just had to brazen it out, that was all. He'd been one step ahead the whole way of the journey, and he wasn't about to let up now. He just had to stick to his story: he couldn't remember anything. They'd all lose interest soon enough, as long as he kept saying that.

Back in Panama Anne was also becoming uncomfortably aware that interest in their story wasn't going to blow over quite so quickly as they'd hoped.

'Mrs Darwin? I just want to ask you a few questions, Mrs Darwin. Can I come in?'

The voice came booming through her door.

Listening on the other side, Anne found herself trembling despite the heat.

Journalists turning up on her doorstep had never been part of the plan. For a moment she thought about closing all the curtains and pretending she wasn't in, but the truth was she was feeling quite lonely. Alone in Panama City, not really knowing what was going on back in London, she had been feeling isolated. And now there was this friendly-sounding man at the door, speaking reassuringly in English. Would it really hurt to let him in?

The voice turned out to belong to a British journalist working in Miami who'd flown to Panama on instructions from the *Daily Mail* in the early hours of Tuesday morning, but had actually received details of Anne's address from the *Daily Mirror* and so was effectively representing both newspapers.

For an hour on Tuesday evening he and a photographer had stood outside Anne's apartment block knocking futilely, as the traffic fumes mixed with the sultry summer air around him. Finally a neighbour had let them into the building but still the journalist had to loiter outside Anne's door, knocking and shouting, his clothes crumpled and dishevelled after the rushed journey.

'Come on,' he muttered under his breath, not at all convinced she was actually there, but knowing it was only a matter of time before the rest of Fleet Street turned up in El Dorado.

At last his persistence paid off.

'What do you want?' came a thin, small voice from the other side of the door.

It was the opening he had been waiting for. Urgently the reporter described to Anne what would happen if she stayed where she was. There was huge media interest in the case, he told her — she'd have people camped outside her door and following her wherever she went; she'd become a virtual prisoner.

She was horrified. She'd only just moved into this apartment block. What would the neighbours think? And how would she cope with people knocking at her door day and night? She was alone in a foreign city.

The persistent British journalist informed her that the best thing she could do was to get right away from her apartment, adding that he'd help her. He'd take her into hiding, somewhere no one would find her and where she'd have time and space to think things through properly. Finally, after about three quarters of an hour of through-the-door negotiation, the door opened and a frightened-looking Anne Darwin stood there, blinking away behind her spectacles at the two strangers in the lobby. Her suitcase was already packed. She'd made a call back to someone in England, she told them, and taken advice. She was ready to go with them.

Put yourself now in Anne's shoes. For years she'd gone quietly about her business, working in the same place, running her home — a grey-haired, anonymous-looking, middle-aged woman. Invisible. Unnoticed. Now suddenly she finds herself at the centre of a media storm. Far from ignoring her in the street, complete strangers are actively seeking her out. More to the point, if these men are to be believed, they're offering large sums of money to find her.

How must it feel to go, in just a couple of days, from a nonentity to a commodity?

So she put her faith in her new journalist acquaintance and let him usher her away, clutching her handbag tightly to her chest as she gazed through the car window at the apartment she'd only just begun to call home.

I'll be back soon, she told herself. This'll turn out to be a flash in the pan.

As the car negotiated the streets of the Panamanian capital she tried to make sense of everything that had happened, but it still seemed impossible. John was supposed to go back and quietly slip back into his old life. How had it happened that they had both become front-page news?

The first hotel they arrived at didn't feel secure, and the mismatched threesome moved to another before finally the reporter felt comfortable asking the questions they'd all been waiting for. By this time Anne had had a long time to anticipate what she was about to be asked, and to think carefully about her responses.

She was delighted that John had reappeared, she told him, describing the phone call from the police station as 'the moment I've always prayed for'.

Asked whether she had any idea he was still alive, she shook her head.

'No, I didn't. I'm as amazed as anyone else.'

As the two talked Anne's interviewer couldn't help noticing how nervous she appeared, but then he couldn't really blame her for that. She'd gone from obscurity to being thrust into the limelight. Little wonder she was finding the whole process rather nerve-racking.

She was open about the financial side of things. Yes, she'd cashed in John's life insurance in good faith when she thought he was dead and she accepted the policies might now have to be paid back. 'If that happens it won't be easy, but I'll deal with it,' she said, her brown eyes liquid with sincerity. In truth she was sincere about this. She'd long accepted that if John really did hand himself in, they'd have to pay back some of the money.

She explained all about her decision to move to Panama. Though some people had been shocked, she'd fallen in love with the place while on holiday and had decided to make it her new home. She described the phone call from Mark telling her that John was alive, and explained how she couldn't drop everything and rush back to England as her furniture was due any minute, but she was hoping to be reunited with her husband just as soon as possible.

Anne Darwin, who'd spoken to no one since dropping her husband off at the airport the Friday before, now talked and talked and talked.

After a few hours, when the weary writer was preparing to file his copy for the late editions of the paper, she even offered to type it for him. Everything was so strange in her life, so turbulent, it felt good to have some company – even if she did have to keep watching what she said. The least she could do was to be helpful. But, even as Anne was expressing her delight and John was rediscovering his sons, a single mother whose small son's nocturnal habits often kept her at her computer at odd hours was idly perusing the Internet. She'd been reading the story of the man who'd paddled out to sea one day and not come back for five years.

Something didn't add up.

The world's a smaller place than we think, the woman, who would always decline to be identified, firmly believed. No one can disappear off the face of the earth for five years without leaving a trace. There had to be some clue somewhere.

Trying to fill that dead night-time, something any lone parent of small children will recognise, the woman started Googling 'John Darwin' and 'Anne Darwin'. She read about how he'd turned up at the police station in central London, she learned how he'd disappeared on a clear, calm day and how his wife had suddenly moved to Panama. Mildly intrigued, she kept going, putting different combinations of key words into the search engine. Chances are he'd have been known by a different name during his 'missing years', she deduced, so she replaced the surname with just 'John', 'Anne' and 'Panama' and opted to search the image bank first.

Keenly she ran her eyes over the thumbnail shots that popped up, twenty to a page. Then suddenly she became completely still. Unable to believe what the tiny image was telling her, she double-clicked to magnify it. And there they were: a youngish, broadly smiling Panamanian relocation agent, standing alongside a grey-haired, bespectacled woman beaming in a toothy but happy way. And beside them, also grinning, albeit in a slightly more subdued, sheepish way, was a middle-aged man who was, without a shadow of a doubt, John Darwin.

The woman sat open-mouthed and stared at the picture: three wide smiles, three contented people, one date – 14 July 2006.

Hardly daring to take her eyes off the screen, she rang Cleveland police.

'You're joking!' exclaimed the man on the other end of the line when told about the photo.

Exactly the same sentiment was echoed by the tabloid paper that was her next port of call.

But it was no joke. The couple, whom the unidentified woman would later nominate for a 'World's Dumbest' award, really had posed for a website photo while the man was supposed to be wandering round without a clue as to his identity and the woman was acting the grieving widow.

The Darwins' carefully constructed house of cards was about to come tumbling down on them, like fruit from a Panamanian palm tree.

In an unidentified hotel, two hours out of Panama City, the journalist who'd tracked Anne down answered his phone just before midnight. It was the *Mirror* newspaper in London.

'I don't believe it,' was his initial response.

Opening up his laptop, he checked his mailbox and found the attachment he'd just been told was coming through. As he double-clicked to download he still couldn't quite believe it was true. It would turn out to be a mistake, he thought, someone else entirely. But when the photo popped up onscreen he could see immediately that it was no mistake: Anne and John Darwin, standing together with the boss of a Panamanian relocation agency, dated the year before – all smiling fit to burst.

For a few long minutes he just gazed at the image. Then he took his laptop over to Anne. 'I've got something to show you,' he told the middle-aged woman with the open, eager-to-please expression. 'The game's up, we know you're lying!'

As she looked at the photo with its toothy smiles and the incriminating date her face drained of all colour as if doused in bleach. For an agonisingly long time she stared in frozen horror at the damning image.

'Have you got anything to say?' she was prompted. But her eyes never left the photo, travelling slowly across the screen. Finally she spoke, her voice faint and tentative: 'I think that picture says a lot, doesn't it?'

She had always had a gift for understatement.

Over the next few hours she opened up to her new best friend in a way that she'd been unable to with anyone over the past four years, but as with so many things in Anne's life, her unburdening was such a hybrid of truth and fiction that it became very hard even for her to remember which was which.

Her revelation of how she'd believed John was dead right up to the moment she opened her front door a year after his disappearance to find him standing on the doorstep was pure fantasy. By contrast, her description of how he then hid himself away, either in the house with her or in the bedsit next door, and the strain that put upon their life together, was all too accurate.

'My family will be devastated by all this,' she sobbed. 'My sons knew nothing, they thought he was dead. Now they're going to hate me!'

Still denying that she had any idea what her husband planned to do when he paddled out in his kayak all those years before, she said she'd been as convinced as anyone else that he was dead and his reappearance in 2003 had placed her in an intolerable position.

What was a loving wife supposed to do? She knew she should have given him up immediately, but he was very persuasive, she explained. She'd tried to get him to turn himself in, but he wasn't having any of it. Besides, she loved him. Which was what had got her into bother in the first place.

'Maybe I just chose the wrong husband,' she lamented aloud.

Again and again the increasingly distraught Anne kept coming back to her sons and the effect all this would have on them. 'They'll probably want nothing to do with me again,' she wailed. 'I can't think why they would want to stick by me now.' She had, she concluded sadly, lost everything and now she was willing to come home to face the music.

It was not a prospect that filled her with relish.

But if Anne thought she had it bad, this was nothing compared to what her newly reinvented husband was going through. When the photo emerged the police lost no time in acting. Shortly before midnight there was a resounding knock at the door of Anthony Darwin's Basingstoke home.

'Mr Darwin,' detectives called through the letterbox after getting no response. 'Come out, we need to speak to you.'

John was in the living room on the phone to Anne when the police burst in.

'You're under arrest for suspicion of deception,' he was told.

As a shocked John gazed blankly around, Anthony was told to go and collect his father's meagre belongings. In a daze he did as he was told and then rejoined the others in the lounge, the tears welling up in his eyes as his father, only so very recently restored to him, was led outside.

'What's happening? What's going on?'

The questions hung in the air long after the police car containing a frightened John Darwin sped away.

The Canoeist Who Came Back from the Dead was under arrest for fraud.

As Wednesday morning broke, with Anne's comments expressing her delight at her husband's miraculous return appearing in the papers, the *Mirror* featured its incredible photo of the Darwins together.

Anthony was the first to see it. At first he just stared at the picture blankly, not comprehending its significance. But gradually all became clear: the grinning couple, the Panamanian estate agent, the damning date printed across the middle: 14 July 2006. While he and Mark had been at home, still mourning their father's loss, his smiling parents were buying up property in exotic locations and planning their retirement funded, it seemed increasingly obvious, by fraudulent insurance claims.

With a growing feeling of nausea he read on, and with each new fact that he uncovered his world shattered further. Other newspapers, left out of the Panama loop, focused on the mounting speculation about the Darwins' financial status — both before and after John's disappearance.

In a frozen, pre-Christmas Britain, desperate for a bit of escapism, the Darwin story captured the imagination of a nation.

Up The Creek Without a Paddle

There was mystery, money and the glamour of foreign travel. Already there were whispers of other women in America that John Darwin had contacted over the Internet before he disappeared.

Everyone, it seemed, had a theory about John Darwin. And everyone wanted to know how the story was going to end, none more so than his shell-shocked sons.

It was left to Anthony to call his brother and tell him about the picture. Mark, like him, was disbelieving at first, then incredulous and then, as the truth of the revelations began to sink in, flooded with wounded outrage.

'We've been lied to!' he sobbed to Flick.

It was just so impossible to take in – the parents who'd loved and protected them had also lied to them, not just once but continuously for years and years. They'd watched them cry for their father and spend hours scouring Internet sites for missing persons or unidentified bodies without saying the words that would have wiped away all their pain.

His father had missed out on Christmases, on Anthony's wedding, on so many important family times – and all for what? For money, for greed, it seemed.

How could this be possible?

At a police press conference detectives read notes from a folder marked 'Lazarus', a nod to the biblical figure who came back from the dead. They'd been most interested to see the photo in the *Mirror* that morning, they said. If it proved genuine, certainly questions would need to be asked.

'I Think I Might Be Missing!'

Meanwhile, back in Panama, normal life seemed to have turned overnight into an action-thriller. After the initial shock of the photo it had become obvious that the Darwin story was now too hot for Anne to be able to remain in Central America. She would have to leave — and fast. But first she had to see her lawyer. First thing Wednesday morning Anne and her journalist consorts appeared at the offices of her attorney in Panama City.

But if they'd hoped to have a quick chat at the offices of Beth Anne Grey, followed by an even quicker exit, they were thwarted by the arrival of a Fleet Street pack that quickly surrounded the building. The situation soon descended into farce with staff from the law firm acting as decoys to lure away the waiting media by driving off at speed in a convoy of black BMWs, each veering off in a different direction.

Still reeling, Anne tried to work out what was going on as she was bundled out of a back exit into yet another black BMW, which then sped away from the scene at breakneck speed. Lying across the back seat of the car, her line of vision level with the leather interior of the car, she was desperate to see what was going on through the window but she also knew she couldn't risk sitting up. Instead she slumped down, listening to the excited voices of the other passengers. Just a few weeks ago she'd been a doctor's receptionist from Hartlepool, going about her business in an ordinary, unshowy way, and now here she was screeching around a Central American city in a getaway car like the President of the United States or a member of the Royal Family. It was just a shame her insides felt so painfully twisted up that she couldn't appreciate the novelty of it all.

Up The Creek Without a Paddle

The fact was Anne Darwin would have given anything to be back at home in Seaton Carew, where, barring the odd kayaking mishap, nothing ever happened. Clearly it was no longer safe for her to be in Panama – everyone wanted a piece of the Darwin pie and the persistent British journalist was not about to start sharing it around. He decided to take his bewildered charge back to Miami.

As Anne gazed out the window of the plane, watching the lights of her adopted home city become ever fainter, she could only wonder to herself again and again: what have I done?

Just to recap, here's how life with the various Darwins stood as Wednesday, 5 December drew to a chilly and rather unsatisfactory close:

John was back on home turf – though not by choice – having been driven from Basingstoke to Kirkleatham police station near Hartlepool, where he would face a medical assessment before being interrogated.

Anne sat in nervous exile in the unlikely setting of Miami, Florida, surrounded by people she hadn't even known 48 hours before, but to whom she now clung as to a lifebelt in the choppy sea.

Mark and Anthony, having briefly gained a father, now faced losing family life as they knew it while news of their parents' double lives began to filter through.

As weeks went, this wouldn't go down as the greatest in the history of the Darwin clan.

13
FACING THE MUSIC

Anne was not enjoying her unplanned visit to the sunshine state. All those months before, when she and John had talked about doing more travelling, seeing more of the world together, this certainly wasn't what she'd had in mind. With John in police custody and her sons not in contact, she had little support as she agonised over headlines in the British press.

They were talking about extradition treaties from Panama.

They were talking about possible jail sentences for fraudsters.

They were talking about applying for passports under false names and stealing identities from dead babies.

Most of all, they were talking about Mark and Anthony.

Tired of the weather and mindless Christmas TV advertising, Britons had come up with a new game to pass the time. It was called 'Did the Sons Know?' Everyone had a different take on whether, and how much, the Darwin boys knew about their father's activities over the past five years.

It was odd, said the doubters, that both boys had left their jobs in the run-up to their father's reappearance. Yes, but then lots of young people change jobs, others countered. Ah, but weren't the properties in the elder son's name? the doubters continued. Yes, but all the money was immediately transferred to their mum in Panama, came the response.

And so it went on.

In some ways Mark and Anthony weren't doing a lot to clear up the situation. Mark had inflamed public curiosity by turning up in the early hours of Thursday morning at his Finchley house-share, from where, according to sensational newspaper reports, he proceeded to remove all his possessions apart from a notebook of instructions for his girlfriend, Felicia Witts.

The notebook, so it was breathlessly reported, contained obscure messages, a poem and coded instructions on how to get to City Airport. There were even hints that it might contain references to Panama.

Both Darwin boys, thin-faced and dark-haired, with telling shadows under wide, sleep-deprived eyes, made a brief reappearance at Anthony's home on Thursday evening to pick up some belongings and then drove away accompanied, apparently, by a police car, but not before they had issued an angry statement to the media.

'How could our Mam continue to let us believe our Dad had died when he was still very much alive?' they asked, declaring themselves 'victims in a large scam' and saying they wanted no further contact with either parent.

The reality was that after nearly six years of mourning both were finding it impossible to come to terms with having regained a father then losing both parents so cruelly and so publicly in the course of just a few short days. Sitting together with Louise and Felicia, the Darwin boys would go over and over what had happened, trying to make sense of it all. They'd mull over occasions from the past years and reconstruct them in the light of what they now knew. Had their dad been watching them while they threw wreaths into the sea on the anniversary of his disappearance? Perhaps he'd been next door all the time when they came back from the inquest?

Over and above the logistical questions of when and where were the 'hows' and 'whys'. *How* had their once-loving father been able to let one of his precious sons get married without attending the wedding? *How* had the parents who had always shielded them from everything throughout their lives put them through such needless misery? *Why* had they believed it was worth sacrificing their family for cash?

It was beyond them. They couldn't understand it, never would be able to work it out. As far as they were concerned it was easier to regard their parents as dead.

Back in Miami, reading reports of her sons' angry words, their mother wrung her sun-freckled hands in misery. How could she have ended up here?

Now her only friends were the reporters assigned by the *Mirror* and the *Mail*. Forlornly she trailed round a shopping mall in the city's Coral Gables district in the company of her minders, idly unfolding, then refolding clothes she had little interest in, still less prospect of wearing.

'I prefer blue colours,' she proffered weakly, trying to pretend this was just an ordinary shopping trip, one she might make with a female friend. 'They're better for my colouring.'

Even while she was making inane chit-chat the nauseous feeling inside her never quite let up, no matter how hard her companions tried to distract her. This wasn't her, this woman on the run, hiding from the world's press, wanted by the police... She was the kind of person who got an illicit thrill from buying a chocolate cream éclair, not jumping in and out of BMWs and on and off planes.

And she'd told so many lies. Anne had started to lose sight of all the lies she'd told. Once she'd made that initial 'confession' about believing John was dead until he turned up on the doorstep a year after he'd vanished, it was impossible to backtrack. Each time she spoke she worried she might say something to contradict herself, exposing herself as a liar and a fraud. And yet how could she possibly tell the truth?

It felt like a bad dream, but she was painfully aware there'd be no waking up from this one, no gradual grateful replacement of the nightmare fantasy with the reassurance of the real world. This was reality now, the constant questions of smiling strangers with their notebooks and their easy sympathy that somehow they seemed to switch on and off as efficiently as their mini tape-recorders.

Like John before her, she found herself stranded in a world with no place to call home. The Panama City apartment was lost

214

to her now, the Seaton Carew houses long sold. She didn't know how to contact her sons or John. Where would she go when she got back to the UK? Whenever she thought of her elderly parents she felt weak with shame. Besides, she couldn't go to stay with them – they had very little room and the pressure of having television crews camping outside their door would be unbearable for them. She'd given up her job and she had no idea how she might go about finding another one.

What would become of her?

Back at the hotel, lonely, miserable and terrified, she poured out her heart to the reporters entrusted with her care. Trying to explain to herself as much as to them how she'd ended up at this sorry point, she went over and over her version of events – the debts, the disappearance.

'I didn't know what he meant to do,' she repeated, as if it were a mantra. 'I really thought he was dead.' In her misery the words spilled from her almost like water into a sinking kayak. 'I'm so sorry,' she sobbed over and over.

She'd never meant all this to happen, she tried to explain. It's just that John had been so very persuasive and then one lie led to another until there were so many lies crowding round her that there was no more room for the truth, and no way out.

She said sorry to everyone – the lifeboat men who'd gone out searching for her husband, the insurance companies who'd paid out for his death, the friends and family she'd deceived. But mostly she was sorry for her sons. 'Misguided as it was, it was done out of love for their father,' she told the reporter from the *Mirror*, begging for understanding.

Up The Creek Without a Paddle

And then she appealed directly to her boys: 'Please believe your Mam when I say I am truly very sorry and I still love you and hope you can find it in your hearts to forgive me.'

John, meanwhile, was belatedly discovering that life as a dead man had had many things to recommend it – freedom, for a start.

At the police station he'd been politely checked over by medical experts and declared fit to be interviewed. Since then there had been nothing but questions. What was his last memory? Did he remember going out in the canoe (pointless to keep correcting it to kayak – he just let it go)? How had the photo come to be taken? What had happened to the insurance money?

It was no longer enough to say that he didn't remember. The photo from the Move to Panama website was proof enough that, unless he'd coincidentally stumbled across his long-lost wife while roaming Central America in the grip of amnesia, he had at some point or other been reunited with Anne before turning up at West End Central police station.

Under the pressure of the relentless questions, slowly but surely his memory started to return.

Here is a couple married for nearly 30 years. For five of those years the husband has been dead. Now, miraculously resurrected, he sits in a police cell in Cleveland, just a short drive away from the prison where he once worked.

His wife, who for the first 50 years of her life never did anything remotely remarkable, is in hiding on the other side of the Atlantic, her only friends those who are being paid to drag her story out of her.

Facing the Music

Their sons have gone to ground.

Here is a family every bit as shattered as the little red kayak that washed up on a Hartlepool beach in April 2002.

Here are four lives that will never be put together again.

Anne's position in Miami was fast becoming intolerable. While in many ways she was anxious to put off her return to England for as long as possible, she knew she couldn't remain for ever in the limbo of shopping malls and hotels, with cups of tea made by people constantly asking her, 'How are you feeling, Anne?', gauging her reactions from one minute to the next in the hope of having something new with which to update their next report.

All of them, minders and 'property' alike, grew restless with the situation. Days seem wearingly long when you're plucked from normal life and thrown together without routine, structure or knowledge of when it's all going to end.

She went for walks in the ritzy areas of the city and trailed around the stores discussing necklines and trouser-cuts with a reporter from the *Mail*. She forced herself to eat and tried to keep her scariest thoughts at bay. Only when the conversation came round to her sons did she lose control. 'How could I have done that?' she'd sob. 'What kind of mother am I?'

She didn't want to think about what would happen to her when she returned to the UK. A couple of times the reporters with her brought up the suggestion that she might face criminal charges, but immediately the shutters came down. She wouldn't think about that, it wasn't possible. Women like her didn't get in trouble with the police, they didn't have to find solicitors and worry about jail sentences. It was unthinkable.

Up The Creek Without a Paddle

She stuck to her story: she'd been a silly, naive woman who'd loved too blindly and let herself become drawn into a situation that was impossible to get out of. She'd hurt people, but she hadn't meant to. She'd stood by her husband, but in so doing had let everyone else down. Now she was sorry, desperately sorry. You might lose friends by making foolish mistakes, but you didn't go to prison, did you?

There was never any question of her not returning to the UK. She had nothing left, she was tired of looking over her shoulder and she wanted to see her family again. And yet the prospect of once more setting foot on English soil filled her with dread. She'd spent her life courting anonymity and she knew she'd be stepping into a spotlight that would be impossible to switch off.

She was only too aware that it was a nightmare that would have to be faced. The only question was when.

While Anne endured her extended dark night of the soul in America's Sunshine State, her home country was in the grip of Darwin mania. The story of the canoeist who'd faked his own death was an early Christmas present of epic proportions for news outlets desperate for a bit of festive cheer. No detail was too skimpy, no news too slight, that it couldn't be endlessly hashed and rehashed in the media frenzy following John's reappearance and arrest.

The papers tracked down Kelly Steele in America, still apparently sleeping with a knife under her pillow after her run-in with him. They talked to Robert Hopkin about how he almost sold the man a catamaran and to Matt Autie, who claimed to have bonded with him over a fishing rod.

Facing the Music

Canoeists and kayakers throughout the country became used to being the butt of everybody's jokes. 'Don't get lost now,' people on land or in passing boats would call out. 'Does your wife know where you are?' Or, everyone's favourite: 'If you're looking for Panama, it's thatta way!'

John's elderly father Ronald, suffering from the after-effects of a stroke, was wheeled out regularly. The old man, who lived just a few miles down the road from his eldest son's new lodgings in Kirkleatham police station, obligingly told stories of how, even as a child, John had always been interested in money and how Anne had cut him out of her life after his son's 'death'.

For a while sleepy Seaton Carew, with its biting North Sea winds and bleak power station vista, rivalled the French Riviera as a magnet for the world's media. The house where the Darwins lived, the bedsit where John hid out whenever his sons came to visit, became sites of pilgrimage for television crews, journalists and interested members of the public, who trooped up and down The Cliff and surrounding roads in search of clues that might unravel the mystery.

The new owner of No. 3 proudly posed with the exposed 'secret entrance' of what was quickly named the 'Tunnel of Love', while his next-door neighbour at No. 4 described in detail the old man who'd shown them round the house.

Again and again John's steps were retraced as he made his fateful journey on 21 March 2002, across the beach and into a sea as smooth as marble. Lifeboat men who'd been on duty that day were called upon to give their opinions on what had happened. Even at the time, one suggested, to the delight of the reporters, it was felt far more likely that he'd turn up in Puerto Banus than anywhere along the Hartlepool coast.

Police interviewed Mark and Anthony as witnesses and not as suspects. After their angry statement cutting all ties with their parents they kept a low public profile, doing their best to steer clear of the probing lenses of the press. Instead the police spoke out on their behalf, declaring them the greatest victims of their parents' scam.

'They have been duped in what can only be described as a really disgraceful fashion,' said Detective Superintendent Tony Hutchison, in charge of the investigation. 'I do feel really, really sorry for them.'

As supermarkets stocked up on brandy butter and cranberry sauce, and the department stores groaned with disorientated Christmas shoppers, the Darwin story seeped into the national consciousness like port spilled on to a white linen tablecloth.

With John behind bars all eyes were on the single player in the drama still at large, still talking openly to the media – Anne Darwin. Was she a misused woman who stood by her manipulative man, or a Lady Macbeth, the real power behind the throne? Everyone had a theory. And everyone was waiting.

Sitting in the departures lounge at Miami Airport on Saturday, 8 December, Anne Darwin certainly didn't feel much like a Criminal Mastermind, or indeed, a Missing Piece in a Jigsaw. Instead she felt very frightened and very, very alone. She knew that the police, after a couple of false alerts, were aware that she would be arriving at Manchester Airport the following day, but she had no idea what they had in mind for her. Nor were the reporters accompanying her home any better informed.

It wasn't a direct flight back, and during the stop-off in Atlanta on that Saturday night she found herself dwelling on everything that had happened and then, worse still, everything to come. Looking around at the other passengers, she longed to switch places with them. They would be met at the airport by loving husbands, wives, children, friends; they'd run into arms thrown wide in welcome. Most of them were holidaymakers or expat retirees, obviously making their way back to the UK for Christmas. She felt a stab of envy, so sharp it was almost physical, as she imagined them unpacking their suitcases in warm, cosy family homes, surrounded by excited grandchildren. Where would she unpack her bag and unfold the clothes far too lightweight for the northern English winter? Shuddering, she imagined setting foot off the plane into the frozen chill of a December morning in Manchester, all the time aware that it wasn't just the prospect of the cold that was making her shiver. What would she do when she landed? Would she make her way to the nearest police station? Would her 'minders' from the press accompany her? Might she, heaven forbid, be arrested at the airport?

Installed at the front of the plane, bound for the frozen north of England, she managed a strained smile as the steward joked, 'Welcome on board this flight for Honolulu!' 'I wish!' she retorted gamely to the reporter by her side.

It was a long, contemplative flight home.

At times she managed to forget the position she was in. She put on her flight socks as normal at the beginning of the flight, knowing that with her history of blood pressure problems and bad circulation she needed to take precautions. Later she dutifully picked away at her chicken supper and reclined her seat back so that she could doze off. But always, just as she began to relax, would come the stark jolt of reality when she'd remember where she was and what might be in store for her.

As the hours passed and the captain announced that shortly they would begin their descent into Manchester, the fears that she had been keeping at bay suddenly came rushing back and her stomach felt tied up in knots.

'I feel sick,' she told her companions, her knuckles white where they clutched the arm of her chair. 'I'm a bag of nerves.'

It was just after 9am on 9 December 2007, and as the plane taxied to a halt, she gazed grimly out the window at the forbidding grey skies, her body rigid with anticipation. For a while there followed that sudden lull that comes at the end of any long plane journey, as passengers allowed themselves to adjust from being airborne and unfettered, members of their own tiny, exclusive community, to being back on the ground and once again engaged with the rest of the world. But before the captain even had time to switch off the seat-belt sign there was a sudden commotion at the front door when the airline staff hauled it open to find a small knot of armed police officers waiting at the entrance.

Clearly taken aback, stewardesses stepped forward to talk to the unexpected visitors, their emphatic whispers hissing down the length of the plane. Then slowly one of them made her way to the tannoy.

'Could Mrs Darwin please come forward?'

It was like something out of a nightmare.

Facing the Music

For a few long, agonising moments she stared straight ahead, as if trying to deny what was happening. If she didn't look up, she thought childishly, she could believe the scrum of police weren't there and this wasn't really happening. It was inconceivable – she wasn't the sort of person who was met off planes by armed policemen, she wasn't a war criminal, or a murderer or a drugs baron. She was a mum of two, a doctor's receptionist; a silly woman who'd made a mistake...

A low-level buzz sounded around the plane as the other passengers whispered urgently to each other, casting furtive glances up and down the cabin. Most had heard of the missing Canoe Widow and were thrilled to find themselves caught up in the whole drama. 'Is that her?' they asked each other, homing in on a flash of silver hair or a pair of prominent spectacles. 'How about that one over there?'

Still Anne sat on, blankly staring at the seatback in front, her skin as grey as a winter's afternoon in Seaton Carew. Slowly she raised herself to her feet and shuffled forward down the aisle of the plane, as if in a trance, clutching her tan handbag and pulling on the jacket that she already knew wasn't going to be warm enough. If ever there was a walk of shame, this had to be it. All around her the passengers were now openly gawping, those at the back standing up for a better view and nudging each other: 'Look, that's her, there she is!'

But the words bounced off her like ping-pong balls as she made her slow progression to the nose of the plane, just a few feet from her seat.

As soon as she reached them the police officers closed around her to read out her rights in low, even voices and to explain that she was under arrest in connection with allegations of fraud.

Arrest. Fraud. Rights.

Which television show had she unwittingly wandered into where such words were bandied about so coolly? For which film villain had she been mistaken?

She didn't belong here, standing solitary at the front. She belonged to the mass of people seated, watching. She belonged to the observers, to the law-abiders, to the ones with nothing to fear. She belonged to those who read the news, not made it, the ones being met by loved ones, not strangers with machine guns.

There's been a mistake; there's been a mistake... There's been a mistake, there's been a mistake... Even while the phrase was going round and round her head like washing on spin cycle, she knew there had been no mistake — apart from the ones she herself had already made.

This was real... This was her and this was now.

Her grey head bowed in shame, she was escorted off the plane.

So here was Anne Darwin. Fifty-five years old, slight of build, quiet of character, being escorted through Manchester Airport by a team of police officers wearing bulletproof vests and sub-machine guns slung over their shoulders. What went through her mind as she was ushered into the airport police station to begin what would be the first in a long series of questionings? How did she feel as she sat for three long hours surrounded by police officers in a place that was home yet was as far removed from it as she had ever been in her life?

Facing the Music

When she finally emerged just after midday she looked as though she had aged ten years since getting off the plane. Her face sagged with the weight of a thousand regrets, her complexion ashen against the gaudy red of her jacket.

As she was bundled into an airport lift she kept her head down, as if the final frayed strings that had been holding it up throughout the long journey back from Panama had just snapped.

If ever there was a woman totally defeated, this was it.

Throughout the 100-mile trip to Hartlepool, as she sat in the back of a black Vauxhall Vectra, escorted by two police cars, Anne reflected on it all: the marriage, the debts, the years of hiding, the impossible dream in Panama... She thought about the sons who had publicly disowned her and the parents she had let down; she wondered what colleagues at work might say when they saw the news, and about how her neighbours would react, had they ever known her at all.

And then she thought about John. He'd won her over, he'd sold her a dream, and when it had all come crashing down he'd brought her down with him.

14
THE WORST CHRISTMAS

There can be few couples in England who spent a more miserable Christmas than the one John and Anne Darwin passed as guests of HM the Queen.

While their peers were cranking up the festive spirit – planning menus with sons and daughters-in-law, trailing round toy shops with wish lists from grandchildren, waking up in the morning thick-headed from the office Christmas party the night before – Anne and John were experiencing their first taste of life on the wrong side of the law.

John had been kept in Kirkleatham police station in Redcar, Teesside, since making the long journey from Basingstoke to Cleveland. Deciding whether or not to charge him, and if so what with, was never going to be easy. After his initial arrest on suspicion of fraud on 5 December, he was brought to Hartlepool, where he was deemed fit for interview by Cleveland police the following day. The initial deadline for questioning, midnight on Thursday 6th, was extended by 12 hours as police struggled to make sense of the increasingly bizarre tale.

On Friday 7th, looking dapper and relaxed in a maroon zipped sweatshirt and chinos, more like a visiting American tourist than an inmate in custody, he strolled into Hartlepool Magistrates Court, which was almost to become a home from home for him over the next few weeks. There he watched impassively as magistrates gave the police powers to hold him for questioning for a further 36 hours.

It wasn't until Saturday, 8 December, when his wife began her long, tortured journey home from the States, that the former teacher, bank worker and prison officer was charged with making an untrue statement to procure a passport and obtaining by deception £25,000 in life insurance from UNAT Direct Insurance Management Ltd. Quite what he made of this is anyone's guess. On the one hand, if you've been kept in for questioning for any length of time there must come a moment when you actually welcome knowing exactly what you're up against, when the relief of the tangible starts to outweigh the possibility of the uncertain. On the other hand, the charges brought with them the end of any illusions he might have been harbouring that the whole debacle would blow over – it wasn't going to go away. It was time for him to start facing up to what had happened, and what might now come to pass.

He dashed off a quick note to the elderly father he had allowed to believe he was dead and who had spent the first year of his disappearance trailing up and down the beach, hoping to find something to tell him what had happened to his son.

The Worst Christmas

'Dear Dad, I'm thinking about you,' he wrote. 'Just a note to let you know you are in my thoughts. Don't worry about anything.'

It was all too late for Ronald Darwin. He'd done nothing but worry about his son since that day in 2002 when he'd dragged a kayak out to sea and not come home again. But for John the enormity of what he'd done was only now really beginning to sink in.

Now it was no longer a game, now it was starting to get serious.

How did he feel as he languished in police custody, aware that the eyes of the world were watching what happened next? Did he, who'd been so many times on the other side of the locked door when working in Holme House, feel ashamed of how low he'd slumped?

Possibly not – you see, John Darwin always had the feeling that he was apart from other men. He aimed higher than they did, pushed forward more barriers.

How many other men of his age, hanging around the pubs of Hartlepool on a Saturday night, could claim to have lived in Central America, or to have owned property in the States? How many of them had thought big enough to follow their dreams instead of just living for the next weekend?

Sure, things hadn't gone exactly as he'd planned, and he had no idea what would happen once he was in front of a court. Plus he hated the idea of Anne having to come back to face a police cell – he knew how private she was and how impossibly hard she'd find it. But, despite all his fears and misgivings, despite his desperation at having found his sons only to lose them again so quickly, he couldn't help feeling a faint glow of pride.

Up The Creek Without a Paddle

It was his face dominating the headlines, his story on everyone's lips. Outside the station he could hear the scrum of reporters whenever the police gave an official statement. It was him they'd come to see. After all the anonymous years spent slogging away in schools or prisons, making instantly regrettable get-rich-quick boasts that never came to anything, finally he was a somebody. Despite everything, a little part of him felt good.

When a humiliated and quivery-lipped Anne finally alighted from the unmarked police car that had driven her on a completely silent journey from Manchester to Hartlepool, she was still in shock. Even the experience of the past few days of being bundled in and out of fast-moving cars to escape the media hadn't prepared her for being photographed at her most tired and vulnerable, crouching down in the back of the car as it pulled up, or being ushered through the back doors of Hartlepool police station, County Durham.

Could it really be just six short weeks since she'd driven away from this place with all its reminders and its anxieties, all its dangerously familiar faces and long memories? She remembered the feeling of liberation as she'd sped off behind the removal van, the exquisite sensation of the smothering cloud pressing down on her over the past few years quite simply lifting off her shoulders. Of course she had felt nervous, but also she remembered the excitement she'd experienced, looking around at the grey, rain-logged buildings and bare, shivering trees, knowing that soon she would be swapping them for sun-drenched terraces and exuberant palms. With every mile she had shed more of her old self, imagining it flaking off piece by piece, carried away by the north-easterly winds, exposing a newer, shinier persona underneath.

And yet here she was again, back in the same streets she'd thought never to call home again, breathing that same dank and damp air. The new self she'd welcomed so happily had deserted her, left behind in a two-bedroom apartment in Panama City along with all the other things she'd no longer need. Meanwhile the old self that she'd so eagerly sloughed off dissolved into a thousand pieces that could never be made whole again.

So what was left? A hollow, frightened woman who'd lost everything she held most dear, and realised too late that she had nothing with which to replace it. Here was a mother whose sons had disowned her, a wife whose husband was locked away from her.

The Anne Darwin who emerged, blinking and bowed, at the Lauder Street entrance to Hartlepool police station at around 2pm on Sunday was a negative imprint of the woman she'd been just days before, an exhausted, depleted shadow who couldn't for the life of her understand how all the steps she'd taken over the past few months, which had meant to lead her to a brave new world, had actually brought her right back to where she started.

That Sunday night John and Anne Darwin sat in police station cells less than ten miles apart, yet it might as well have been the Atlantic separating them.

By this time John had had a chance to become accustomed to his new, somewhat curtailed circumstances, but he was brooding about what would happen the following day, when he was due to appear at Hartlepool Magistrates Court. Even though his solicitor had talked him through the whole procedure, he was understandably nervous about the logistics, particularly the knot of reporters waiting outside for him, a fox about to be released before a rabble of hunting dogs.

While he was concerned about what might happen to him, he wasn't exactly uncomfortable. To be fair, life in Seaton Carew during his 'dead' period hadn't been dissimilar to being locked up in Kirkleatham, so the physical confinement didn't come as too much of a shock.

Anne, on the other hand, was terrified. Growing up, she'd been the perfect daughter, the one who never did anything wrong. She'd attended convent school, married a suitable man, been a good wife and a devoted mother. She didn't belong here. Surely they'd realise that they'd made a mistake? And yet she knew that the only mistakes were the colossal blunders she'd made herself. For the first time in her life she was starting to realise that criminals weren't a separate class of person, but maybe, just maybe, they were a little bit like herself and John, good people who'd made bad choices.

On her arrival at Hartlepool police station a doctor was called to give Anne a quick health check before she was shown into a cell for the night. Glancing over at her pallid complexion and shell-shocked, staring eyes, police officers exchanged knowing looks. They'd seen this kind of expression before – the fear of the first-time visitor, the nervous glances round the interior, the endless wringing of hands... But usually the look was worn by parents of offenders, people who'd never imagined setting foot in a police station apart from to report a suspicious person or hand in a lost bag, and who couldn't for the life of them work out what had brought them here. You'd see them gazing around in bewilderment, wondering when they would wake from this nightmare.

For Anne Darwin the nightmare was only just beginning.

The whole of that first night she struggled to sleep. She longed for the oblivion of unconsciousness, but the knowledge of her situation, combined with the effects of her long journey, made that particular escape impossible. Instead images flashed, unwanted, through her mind – her sons, gaunt-faced with worry, hiding their shame behind closed doors while a policeman told the world on their behalf how deeply they'd been hurt by the very people they thought would always protect them; passengers on the plane, their eyes wide with gleeful horror at the sight of the machine guns, already rehearsing in their heads the story they'd tell to those who came to meet them; the speeding cars, the silent police escorts, the sight of her own gormlessly grinning face on the front pages of the newspapers; the reporters with their heads cocked in studied sympathy, fingers permanently hovering over the pause button on their tape machines. Once so orderly, her life had become a slide show of ever-more chaotic vignettes in which nothing made sense and the only constant was her ever-dissolving self.

The following morning she was more hollow-eyed and pale than ever. After a meal, as the sky bled anaemically from sludge to grey, questions began in earnest.

If she thought she'd become used to answering queries after her time with her press entourage she was much mistaken. The past few days had been just a rehearsal – the real interrogation started now. Still, she stuck to the story she'd given the newspapers: she hadn't known John had faked his own death; she'd applied for insurance money in good faith and been shocked when he turned up on her doorstep, a year after his 'disappearance'.

By this stage it had been just over a week since the Darwins had last seen each other, yet so much had happened since that fateful goodbye at Panama City Airport it was as if years had passed. But any hopes of a tearful reunion were swiftly dashed.

The next day, John was brought yet again to Hartlepool Magistrates Court. It stood on Victoria Road, just yards from the police station where Anne was being questioned, but it might as well have been on a different continent because the couple were kept well apart.

Did she, at the beginning of the long day of questioning in the police station, glance at the windows, at the unwashed December sky, and wonder if each car engine signified her husband's arrival? Did John, knowing where Anne was likely to be, draw strength from her proximity, even though the doors between them remained resolutely shut?

Certainly John looked more agitated than he had for a while as he waited to be led into the dock to listen to the charges against him. Before he entered, wearing the same maroon tracksuit and chinos, a court usher asked three times if any relatives were present, but his question was met with silence from the assembled crowd of journalists and police. During John's four-minute appearance in the dock the cockiness that had been in evidence before was discernibly muted. Instead he stared around the courtroom with slightly bewildered eyes, speaking only to confirm his name and date of birth before being remanded into custody once again until the following Friday. No application was made for bail.

Not surprisingly, given John's proven talent for disappearing, the Prosecutor commented afterwards that had bail been demanded she would have opposed it. Afterwards he was taken to his new home at Durham Prison and it was left to his solicitor, John Nixon, to describe to reporters how his client was asking anxiously for news of his wife and begging for reconciliation before their 34th wedding anniversary on 22 December. 'He is desperate to see his wife, to be reunited with her. He is anxious to know about her well-being... He is anxious for everything to be resolved,' he stated.

For Anne, behind the closed doors of Hartlepool police station, resolution, like Christmas cheer, seemed a hopeless dream.

For the whole of that miserable Monday the doctor's receptionist hung her head and wept softly as she talked about her estranged sons during breaks in questioning. By now she had reached rock bottom and she no longer really cared what happened to her, but she was desperate to be reunited with her children, to know that she hadn't really lost everything, that there was still some part of her life that remained intact.

That evening, exhausted and haggard, she was charged with two counts of deception. The first related to the same £25,000 life insurance payout John had also been charged with, and the second related to the £137,000 mortgage paid off by Norwich Union after the April 2003 inquest.

When it was explained to Anne that she would have to appear at Hartlepool Magistrates Court the following morning to be officially remanded into custody, she felt sick. She knew she wouldn't have to do anything except confirm her name and date of birth, but the thought of standing up in a courtroom in the very community where she'd built up a respectable reputation over all those years, only to be charged with fraud, filled her with shame and self-loathing.

The patients at Gilesgate Medical Centre, where Anne had worked all those years, would never have recognised the woman who stood before Hartlepool JPs on Tuesday, 11 December. In place of the calm, unruffled receptionist who'd juggled waiting lists and appointments with courteous control was a shaky, visibly distressed ghost of a figure who answered the two questions put to her in a faint, almost whispering voice.

The five-minute hearing seemed to last an eternity as Anne, dressed in a cream zip-up cardigan and black trousers, struggled to maintain her composure. As the charges against her were read out she stifled a gasp. It was real, it was happening. Nothing was going to stop it.

She could barely focus on the proceedings as the court heard the Prosecutor oppose bail on the grounds that she might abscond, and the Chairman pronounced the case serious enough to merit a Crown Court hearing.

Please tell me this isn't happening, chanted a voice inside her head. *Please tell me this is a mistake.*

The Worst Christmas

When she was remanded into custody until 10.20am the following Friday it barely registered. Suddenly she was being handcuffed to a female security guard, wincing as she felt the metal close around her wrist. She'd seen it on countless detective shows, but never in a million years could she have imagined that one day she would be led out of a courtroom in shackles.

As she arrived at Low Newton Remand Centre in Durham, not far from Durham Prison, where John had been taken, her solicitor, Nicola Finnerty, told the press how much her client longed to see her sons: 'The most upsetting aspect of this whole thing for her is the effect it has had on her sons. After all, she is their mother.'

Commenting on her client's obvious distress, she described her as 'very tired and very emotional'. No one who'd seen Anne's red-raw eyes, with their encircling dark rings, would have been surprised to learn from Ms Finnerty that her client had been 'very tearful'. 'If her sons would like to see her then she would love to see them or hear from them,' the solicitor appealed.

From her cell Anne penned a letter to each of her sons in her careful if childish writing.

'I can't begin to imagine how you must be feeling,' she told them. 'All I can do is apologise and hope that one day you will find it in your heart to forgive me & Dad.'

Each letter was as painful to write as if she were scratching the words across her very flesh. But if she was hoping her entreaty might soften the hearts of the sons who'd publicly denounced her, had she waited in hope of an unexpected visitor being announced, she was to be disappointed.

Mark and Anthony showed no sign of weakening in their resolve to cold-shoulder the parents who'd lied to them and duped them, watching them grieve unnecessarily for nearly six long years for a father who at times was just a few feet away.

After their statement condemning what their parents had done and insisting they wanted nothing more to do with them, the brothers kept a low profile although police revealed they had been in regular contact. Now that both parents were in custody their reluctance to appear in the spotlight became even more pronounced and they instructed solicitors to be present for any future police interviews, despite officers being at pains to emphasise their status as witnesses rather than suspects.

Meanwhile Darwin mania continued to rage unabated throughout the world's media. With a few days' lull in the legal proceedings in Hartlepool, journalists looked for other ways of feeding the public appetite with new angles on the couple dubbed 'The Canoe Two'. In the absence of any feedback from either Darwin son the bewildered families of Mark's girlfriend and Anthony's wife were hounded for comments.

Meanwhile, desperate for news, the grateful press leapt upon any developments in the story, no matter how tenuous. When, overnight, a yellow-and-black road sign appeared on a main road into Seaton Carew reading, 'Welcome to Seaton Canoe – twinned with Panama', it made the news across the world.

It was left to a rather sheepish-looking spokesman from Hartlepool Council to explain that, actually, Seaton Carew was part of Hartlepool and therefore twinned with Huckelhoven, near Cologne in Germany.

The Worst Christmas

'We have no plans to twin with Panama City just yet,' he added solemnly.

On the Internet John Darwin T-shirts bearing logos such as 'John Darwin School of Canoeing, Hartlepool to Panama' proved a surprise pre-Christmas hit on auction website eBay.

With the rest of the news dominated by the tragic faces of Madeleine McCann's parents, who faced the grim prospect of their first Christmas without their missing daughter, the story of the kayaker who tried to come back from the dead provided welcome light relief and, just like the man at its centre, nobody would let it die.

By Thursday 13th, the day before both Darwins were due to appear once again before Hartlepool Magistrates, this time via video link, the papers had got wind of John's brief and not very illustrious career as an American property speculator, although it would be a few days before the full story of Kelly Steele's ordeal by Darwin became public.

There was also mounting speculation about the motivation behind John's seemingly bizarre decision to abandon his fledgling new life abroad and return to England to hand himself in. One paper claimed to have talked to a prison inmate who'd befriended John at Kirkleatham police station and been told that he'd come back because Anne was having an affair and was set to leave him with nothing.

This wasn't the first time that the notion of infidelity on Anne's part was behind John's surprise reappearance had been mooted. For some observers there could be no other feasible explanation. After all those years of sacrifice, cooped up in a bedsit next door to his home, finally he was reaping the rewards – the new home overseas, exciting new business venture, lots of money in the bank... What could have made him come back, if not for her pulling the financial rug out from under his feet, people speculated.

With the only two people who knew the full story languishing in prison out of reach, there could be no definitive answers.

Friday, 14 December was a busy day for Hartlepool Magistrates Court. That morning both John and Anne Darwin made brief appearances via video link on charges of deception. John had finally changed out of his maroon tracksuit top and was sporting a light-blue shirt and blue jeans. His wife, who always opted for comfort over style, was wearing a grey sweatshirt with black trousers. Both were ordered to remain in custody over the Christmas recess before facing magistrates again on 11 January.

They would be just four miles apart, but never had the Darwins been so lost to each other. While John's solicitor revealed he'd put in a special request to see his wife but had been denied, Anne remained resolutely silent, making no mention of wishing to be reunited with her husband.

Now the newspapers went into overdrive. Every titbit of news about the 'Cleveland Couple' was leapt upon like a new consignment of Wii's, that year's Christmas must-have, which was flying off the shelves just as quickly as stocks were replenished.

Kelly Steele became the 'Kansas City Housewife' who lived in fear of 'Darwin the Druid'. Obligingly she posed for photos and shared details of the terror she'd been living in since her brush with the 'Crazed Canoeist'.

The Worst Christmas

Tabloid journalists scoured the sex clubs of Panama City to find anyone who would admit to seeing the infamous 'Death-Faker' hanging around the parts of the capital not featured in any tourist brochures. Several club owners and staff at the seedier bars claimed to have seen Darwin during the time that he was waiting for Anne to join him.

It appeared to be open season on Mr Canoe.

Christmas hadn't been the easiest of periods in the Darwin family since John went missing, but as far as dismal festivities went, the Christmas of 2007 made the years before it seem like a Hollywood feel-good movie.

Anne sat slumped in her cell, going over and over what had happened. Anyone who has ever undergone a truly traumatic experience will know how easy it is to torture yourself by trying to consciously work your way back in time to the moment when the first bad decision was made, as if getting back there can somehow unlock the past, enabling you to slip back inside and make the other choice, to take the other fork in the road.

When was it that things started to go so horribly wrong? Was it when she made the call to report John missing or when he first mooted the idea of staging his own death? Or did the rot set in even earlier, when they made that fateful decision to buy the two houses in Seaton Carew?

Alone with her thoughts and her regrets, Anne replayed scenes from her past, changing the dialogue in her mind so that where she'd initially agreed, or gone along with something, now she refused, standing firm in the face of all threats and persuasion, experiencing the satisfaction of knowing she was sticking to her principles.

Whenever she saw her solicitor she'd ask if there had been any word from the boys and then shrink back into herself at the inevitable shaking of the head, not needing to hear the word 'sorry'. Still she continued to deny all involvement in the fraud. She hadn't had a clue that her husband was planning such a thing, she insisted, and she'd been so shocked when he turned up on her doorstep. Of course she'd applied for that money in good faith. Her only crime had been blind loyalty.

But then all that changed.

The turnabout came after Anne and John were permitted to speak by phone to mark their 34th wedding anniversary. Whatever was said between the two of them clearly gave Anne some food for thought because a few days later, having been confronted with John's library card in the name of John Jones, showing he'd been in Hartlepool just weeks after his disappearance, she decided to confess.

'I knew the day John had gone missing that he had gone missing, and that he'd planned it,' she admitted in her soft, slightly hesitant Durham accent. Her voice was calm but slightly distant, as if recalling a dream.

As her version of events shifted, so too did the angle of her defence. No longer was she claiming that ignorance had led her to this situation, now the blame was laid squarely on John. He'd bullied her into taking part in this wild scheme against her will and better judgement.

It was to become known as a defence of 'marital coercion'.

Christmas for all the Darwins was a washout.

The Worst Christmas

If Anne could have slept through Christmas Day she would have. Nothing about it, from the flaccid canteen vegetables to the token strands of tinsel, bore any resemblance to Christmases gone by. Everything was wrong and she begin to see how it would ever become right again.

Nor were Mark and Anthony exactly full of festive goodwill as Christmas drew inexorably closer. On Christmas Eve, which fell on a Monday, affording many workers a much-appreciated extra day off, Anthony's mother-in-law, Shelley Tilley, told of her health concerns for Anthony and his wife Louise. 'They have lost half a stone each,' she confided to reporters. 'It has been very, very stressful.'

The brothers might have been forgiven for being lacking in Christmas spirit when you consider just how much had happened to them. Within the space of two months they'd lost a mother to the lure of Panama, gained a father they thought they'd lost, then lost both parents again in a very public and shameful manner. As they themselves described it, they had been on 'an emotional rollercoaster'. You couldn't blame them then, could you, for being ever so slightly bah humbug-ish about the whole thing?

And what of John, by Anne's account the mastermind of the whole operation?

Just a few short weeks earlier, he had been planning to spend Christmas in a penthouse flat in Panama, lounging on the terrace, his only worry being how soon he should reapply Factor 30 to his balding head. So what must it have been like to look round his cramped prison cell and know that he might not see the sun for a

243

very long time? How heavily must the gloom of a north-east winter have pressed down on him?

Imagine the complete antithesis of an upmarket, sun-flooded modern apartment in Central America in the height of summer and you're probably thinking about something close to Durham Prison, or Old Elvet as it is also known. Built in 1810 and home to many notorious prisoners over the years, it's an imposing, monolithic, resolutely gloomy building, its ground floor said to be haunted by the ghost of a prisoner killed in his cell by another inmate.

Though the infamous She Wing, which once housed female Category A prisoners such as Rose West and Myra Hindley, has been closed, and the prison downgraded to a Category B local prison, Old Elvet remains an oppressive, cheerless place which, in the year John disappeared, had the dubious honour of boasting the highest suicide rate of any prison in England.

Armed robber turned man of letters John McVicar managed the impossible when he escaped from the Maximum Security Wing in 1968, but it's fair to say that, after travelling halfway round the world to hand himself into the authorities, the idea of escape was a long way from John Darwin's mind.

Did he spend his time locked up tearing himself apart with regrets and self-recrimination? Was he pacing his cell, driving himself crazy with memories of the life he'd thrown away and far-off Christmases when the Darwins were a family rather than a national joke? One can only speculate. But since self-awareness had never been John's strongest suit, one might be forgiven for suspecting the answer to be a categorical 'no'.

The Worst Christmas

What's more likely is that he got through Christmas in the same way as his fellow inmates might have done — by focusing on the here and now and trying not to think too hard about what had gone before, or worse by far, what was yet to come.

15
SUNK!

January 2008 was a bumper month for resolutions. Not only were people ditching smoking in their droves, prompted in part by Britain's new anti-smoking laws that consigned them to shivering on pavements outside pubs and workplaces, but also, with a whiff of recession in the air, there was a palpable tightening-of-belts mentality. People were definitely in the mood for giving things up.

Of course prison isn't the easiest place for New Year's resolutions. What's the point in giving things up when you need all the cheer you can get? Besides, if something's interesting enough to be a vice, it's like gold dust in a place where time hangs so heavily.

For Anne Darwin the only resolution she could focus on was a resolution to her current nightmare situation: she wanted to get out of prison.

John's attitude was more phlegmatic. The reality was that prison was much less of a shock for him than his law-abiding wife. Don't forget that he'd worked in the prison service for years, turning up day after day to patrol landings where the noise of metal upon metal and male voices echoing along halls permeated his very soul. And hadn't he been living in a semi-prison during those four years of hiding away in Seaton Carew?

In truth prison was somewhere John felt if not at home, at least at ease. In Durham he'd been given his own single cell, a rare privilege, where he could hide away from company if he chose. However, he'd become something of a celebrity in the prison, and he found the other prisoners sought him out – something of a novelty for a man who'd often found it hard to make friends.

Even the warders stopped to have a joke with him.

'Don't be getting on that rowing machine,' they'd tell him when it was his turn in the gym. 'We don't want you getting away!'

He passed his time playing pool or chatting with the other inmates on his block. Unaccustomed to blokey chit-chat, he nevertheless soon cottoned on to the universal male truth that raising your eyes to the skies, shaking your head and muttering the word 'women' is an acceptable answer to almost any awkward question. Word soon went round that Mr Canoe was behind bars largely because he'd been shafted by Mrs Canoe.

'She had another man,' they whispered to one another. 'She'd have left him with nothing.'

When he wasn't socialising John would sit in his cell bent over a notebook, pen in hand, replying to some of the huge volume of letters he was sent, many of them from women intrigued by the man who'd tried to take on the system – and so very nearly won. He had always liked to think of himself as something of a ladies' man and he relished these flirtatious exchanges.

Of course, as January sluggishly spluttered into life, and the nation's courts shook off their hangovers and went back to business as usual, his relative equanimity started to waver. He knew, as did everyone else, that more charges would be brought against him. So far he and Anne had each been charged with two crimes, but he was sure there was more to come. There was the payout from his prison pension scheme to account for plus, in his case, the rest of the life insurance money, so there was little doubt that he'd be going back to court. The one bright spot on the horizon was the prospect of seeing Anne there.

Since before Christmas he had been trying to arrange to see his wife without success. Their wedding anniversary had come and gone with a stilted telephone call, but without any reunion, as they languished in their respective cells, just a few miles apart. Then Christmas and New Year had arrived, and all the time he'd been unable to see her. But their joint appearance in Hartlepool Magistrates Court on 9 January was a chance to find out how she was coping, what she'd been saying and, most of all, how much she blamed him for all that had happened.

But if he'd been hoping for a Hollywood-style reunion he was to be very much disappointed. His first glimpse of Anne was through a glass partition as they waited to be admitted to the courtroom. She was wearing a light-blue jacket in her favourite zip-up style and he could see clearly the toll that the past few weeks had taken on her. When he'd said goodbye to her back at the apartment in Panama

City (how long ago that now seemed) she'd been relaxed and lightly tanned after their holiday in Costa Rica, the sunlight reflecting brightly off the flecks in her brown eyes. But the Anne he saw through the glass that January morning was pale and drawn, the lines on her face pleating her skin like a paper fan. As they caught each other's eye she mouthed something to him but, partially deaf at the best of times, he had no hope of hearing her through the glass divide.

Ushered into the courtroom, they stood awkwardly side by side, each of them flanked by a dock officer. John, who had dressed carefully in black leather jacket, cream jumper and blue shirt, took his cue from his set-mouthed wife and stared straight ahead, making no attempt to talk to her as the proceedings got underway. Only when asked to confirm his name and age did he speak, his voice sounding gruff and strange in the unnatural hush of the packed courtroom.

The two were charged with four further counts of obtaining money by deception: £25,186 from Capita Hartshead Teachers' Pension Scheme, £58,845 from Capital Hartshead Civil Service Pension Scheme, £2,000 from the Department for Work & Pensions Bereavement Benefit Scheme and £2,273 from the Department for Work & Pensions Bereavement Benefit Scheme.

John was charged with a fifth count of dishonestly obtaining £137,000 from Norwich Union Life Services – the same charge that had already been laid against Anne.

The figures, random and obscene, seemed to take for ever to be read in court, where, to the Darwins, each second lasted hours. Huge sums of money seemed to echo in the air long after the speaker had finished.

Sunk!

To Anne's cringing Catholic ears each word seemed to carry the
same hidden accusation: Greed, Greed, Greed. Standing to her
right, John inclined his head towards her so that he could hear
through his one good ear, but he didn't raise his eyes up to hers,
just inches away, instead keeping them fixed on the floor or staring
straight ahead.

What was it he feared seeing in her gaze? Did he feel he'd go to
pieces if he locked eyes with the woman to whom he'd been
married for 34 years and alongside whom he now faced the
greatest challenge of their lives? Or could he already, from
standing so close to her, sense the weight of reproach he'd find in
her eyes – a blame so strong and vivid it had become a living force
which squeezed in between them, crushing against him so that he
shrank imperceptibly away?

Or could it be that there really had been a rift that prompted
John Darwin to head for home, and this remained unhealed, with
unspoken resentments still dancing in the frosty air between them?

Whatever the reasons the Darwins, or 'Mr and Mrs Canoe' as
they were now more familiarly known to the nation, endured
their brief court hearing as if they were solitary defendants,
alone in the dock, neither acknowledging the other's presence as
they were informed that they'd be remanded into custody once
more to appear again before the court via video link on 18
January. The committal date for transferring the case to Teesside
Crown Court was set for 15 February. Neither solicitor entered
any pleas to the charges.

As they were led out of the dock, there was no attempt at eye
contact between the two prisoners, no tentative calling-out of

251

names or comforting glances. John and Anne may have chalked up nearly three and a half decades of marriage, but they might as well have been strangers.

How do you fill your days when you're locked up in prison, living from one court appearance to the next? The gaps between solicitor's visits stretch yawningly wide when there's nothing else to punctuate the tedium – no calls from worried sons, no point in reading when the words of the book just dance before your eyes and you suddenly realise you've read that same paragraph ten times before.

Anne found the days in prison dragged like wellington boots through mud. There was too much time to dwell on what had gone before, too much time to worry about what was to come. She and John faced very serious charges. If she had fooled herself before about just how much trouble they were in, she certainly knew the truth now. Already possible prison sentences of up to ten years had been bandied about. She'd be 65, the prime of her middle years lost to her.

Would she have a family to come out to? Would she have money and somewhere to live?

John, meanwhile, busied himself with his flirty correspondence. One female pen pal, who would later generously share her letters with a Sunday tabloid, received a mathematical equation written on notepaper, giving the formula by which she could work out the size of Mr Canoe's equipment – and from the context of his letter, he wasn't referring to his kayak and paddle!

Asked by the woman if he and Anne had an open relationship,

John apparently replied 'not at the moment' but added insightfully that one never knew what might happen in the future.

On 18 January, as scheduled, the Darwins once more appeared before Hartlepool Magistrates Court, this time via separate video links, to hear that they'd been remanded into custody again. By this stage the court appearances had become almost routine fixtures in their lives and, if not a welcome break from the monotony of prison life, at least a way of punctuating the days that seemed to stretch so endlessly ahead.

Nor was there any more fanfare on 15 February, when the couple again appeared briefly by video link to hear their case being officially transferred for trial to Teesside Crown Court, which heard the more serious cases.

Anne, this time in a grey sweatshirt, appeared even more tired than ever as she once more confirmed her name and date of birth. Worry had etched extra years into her face, causing the flesh round her down-turned mouth to pucker and sag like an overused dishcloth.

Then, 25 minutes later, it was John's turn. Wearing a green sweater over a blue shirt, he also spoke only to confirm his name and age, his face impassive over the video monitor. Again no plea was entered on either's behalf, nor an application for bail.

Had they by now become inured to the shame of appearing before JPs? Perhaps repeated exposure to the Magistrates Court, to the often grinding tedium of the mechanics of the legal process, had hardened them to the implications of what was happening to them? Or did Anne, after being escorted back to her cell, sit on the edge of her bed and put her weary head in her hands and feel her whole body shake while the magistrate's words echoed round in her head?

She didn't have much experience of legal matters, but even she knew the difference between a Magistrates and a Crown Court, between a misdemeanour and a serious crime.

It meant that she was in serious trouble.

Can any period of time drag any slower than the interval between being charged with a crime and facing trial?

Once again Anne was living in limbo – in prison but not yet condemned.

Low Newton Prison, about four miles out of Durham, is an all-women institution, housing a mixture of remanded and sentenced prisoners. Built in the 1960s, it has none of the gothic austerity of Durham Prison, which John was slowly learning to call home. As prisons go, Low Newton is pretty relaxed and not too intimidating; it has been commended for fostering respect between staff and the 300-odd prisoners. Even so, Anne found the routine of institutional life almost impossible to adjust to.

While John revelled in his status as celebrity prisoner, obligingly signing autographs for released pals, Anne couldn't bring herself to make light of her situation. Though friendly and warm to other prisoners, just as she had been to patients at the doctor's surgery, she found herself shrinking more and more into herself, zipping up her fears like one of her cosy cardigans.

Her face, which just a few short weeks before had gazed back at her relaxed, sun-kissed and radiating vitality, from the bathroom mirror in her Costa Rican hotel room, now appeared sunken and deflated, like a punctured balloon. It was not the face of someone about to make light of their circumstances.

Outside the prison, however, it was a different story. In the absence of new information the media and interested observers kept Darwin mania alive by thinking up new trivia. Readers were reminded that the saying 'A Man, a Plan, a Canal, Panama' was a palindrome – in other words, it read the same backwards as forwards. New jokes were invented or old ones adapted with the Darwins in mind. Anne Darwin and a friend go to the police station to report her husband missing, went one such joke. Asked for a description, she describes him as 30 years old, 6 foot tall and fit as a butcher's dog. 'But John's 57 and bald,' the friend protests but is silenced by Anne's reply: 'Yes, but who wants that loser back?'

Another joke had John going for a medical check-up only to be told by the doctor: 'Bad news, I'm afraid. You've got amnesia and you're technically dead.' To which Darwin replied: 'Well, at least I'm not technically dead.'

Nobody, it seemed, could get enough of the Darwins and their story of greed, escape and, seemingly, abject stupidity.

Hartlepool was enjoying its moment in the spotlight. Up until then the town had been chiefly famous for the legendary monkey-hanging incident, which supposedly took place two centuries before. It was during the Napoleonic Wars, and the people of Hartlepool were primed to expect a French invasion from the sea. When one morning a bedraggled pet monkey, obviously a survivor from a shipwreck off the coast, was washed up on shore it was immediately arrested on suspicion of being a French aggressor. The monkey was tried, and when it failed to give an adequate account of itself it was convicted of being a French spy, sentenced to death and hanged without further ado.

Faced with a choice of being known as 'The Town Which Hanged a Monkey Because They Thought It was a French Spy', or 'The Back-From-the-Dead Canoeist Town', the people of Hartlepool decided there was no competition and John Darwin was enthusiastically adopted as the town's unofficial mascot.

As 2008 inched its way towards spring, both Darwins struggled with the monotony of daily prison routine. Some prisoners have been known to hold ant races to relieve the tedium of life behind bars, but John Darwin found a different way of passing the interminable hours. In a faint echo of the garden gnomes that he used to make, Mr Canoe began fashioning sculptures from matchsticks. One of his first efforts – a kayak made from thousands of matchsticks stuck together and then finely sanded – was presented to a departing prisoner as a leaving gift, flamboyantly signed by its maker.

It's funny how working with your hands can clear the mind. During the many hours that John spent hunched over his new hobby he had plenty of time to think about the events that had led him to this point and, above all, about the forthcoming hearing at Leeds Crown Court. He knew there could be no question of pleading not guilty; the evidence against him was just too overwhelming. And though he still showed traces of his old customary arrogance, the weeks in prison and the rejection by his sons and, lately, by his wife had taken their toll, and he no longer assumed he could outwit the system.

Sunk!

Sometimes in the dark heart of the night, when there was no one around to try to impress and he allowed himself to linger too long on the mess he'd made and the bleakness of his future, despair would flood through him like a scream and he'd crack his head against the cell wall, or grab the sharpest thing that he could find and score marks into his arms. In a strange way the physical pain seemed to distract him temporarily from the torment of his thoughts. For a few blissful minutes he'd concentrate only on the discomfort in his arms, or the throbbing of his head, but all too quickly the awareness of his own hopeless situation would return and he'd squeeze his eyes shut in desperation.

He knew he was facing a prison sentence. The only question was: how long?

Anne spent all the time she could huddled with her lawyer. How many times over the past few weeks had she regretted the interviews she gave to the newspapers and wished she'd had more time to think things through? She'd been in such a state, she explained, everything had been so jumbled up in her mind. She hadn't been thinking properly.

If only she'd been a little more circumspect and given herself a chance to prepare what she was going to say maybe she wouldn't be feeling quite so anxious about the upcoming court case and, more importantly, perhaps she wouldn't have lost the support of her sons.

While John whittled away in his cell, Anne paced the floor in hers, going over and over the events of the past few years. It hadn't been her fault, she kept telling herself: it was John who was to blame. He'd always thought himself a cut above other people; he'd always been so hard to say no to. Oh yes, she'd made her mistakes, some whopping ones, but in the end surely any court would see that her greatest crimes were naivety and foolish loyalty?

Heads close together, their voices a constant low murmur, she and her lawyer worked on.

Leeds Crown Court, a modern building made of sand-coloured brick, stands lumpily a couple of blocks to the north of the River Aire, on the corner of Crown Street and New York Street. It probably wouldn't make any sightseeing list for visitors to the city, but to John and Anne Darwin, whose worlds had suddenly shrunk to the size of their prison cells, even this unsympathetic civic structure represented a welcome expansion of their sour and oppressive reality as they turned up there, on 13 March, for their pre-trial hearing.

Anne, wearing a cream cardigan, white shirt and dark trousers, looked like she should be handing out library tickets, not facing charges that, if proven, would see her put in prison for a very long time. John, more casual in a black leather jacket over a blue shirt and jeans, tried to squeeze her hand as they stood side by side in the dock. Staring fixedly ahead, she didn't respond.

Very few people expected the Darwins to plead anything except guilty at this hearing. They'd listen to the charges, chant their mea culpas, then be sentenced, so avoiding the need for a full-blown trial. The facts spoke for themselves – those and Anne's partial confessions to the newspapers. Their best hope, most agreed, was to hold their hands up and hope for a lenient judge.

Sunk!

True to expectation, John, looking suddenly far smaller than he had in previous appearances, as if prison had somehow shrunk him to a scaled-down model of his former self, and reading from a piece of paper on which his pleas were written, pleaded guilty to seven charges of obtaining cash by deception and one passport offence. He denied six charges of deception and nine of using criminal property. Peter Makepeace, the counsel who had been instructed to act for John once the case passed from Magistrates Court to Crown Court, informed the court that he accepted a 'lengthy custodial sentence' was 'inevitable'. He also referred, intriguingly, to 'self-harming issues' surrounding John's stay in prison.

Just like his boat, it seemed Mr Canoe had taken rather a battering.

It was left to his wife to stage the greatest upset of the day.

'Not guilty,' she answered to each of the charges, in her soft but steady voice. 'Not guilty... Not guilty.'

Fifteen times she repeated the same flat phrase, in her soft, flat voice. Quite simply, she denied the lot. The quietly spoken doctor's receptionist, who'd always gone to church and never made a fuss, was determined not to go down without a fight.

She would have to stand trial.

And back they went, to their respective prisons, to resume their torturous waiting game. Only now, for the first time, they weren't in this together. For John it was over. All he had to look forward to was being told the length of his prison sentence, which would happen after the verdict in his wife's trial. For Anne, however, it

Up The Creek Without a Paddle

was a different story. On 14 July 2008, at Teesside Crown Court, it would be sink or swim for Mrs Canoe.

16
THE CASE THAT DIDN'T HOLD WATER

Spring 2008 edged hesitantly into summer with very little discernible sign of change. Disaffected English supporters – their team hadn't got through the qualifiers – watched from the sidelines as Spain romped to victory in the European Championship, the UK's growing knife culture claimed a clutch of fresh victims, and across the country the usual assortment of fêtes and wedding parties were held under makeshift shelters as the weather performed its traditional pendulum trick, swinging wildly between sunshine and downpours.

From Anne Darwin's prison cell the changing of the seasons, once viewed in panoramic glory through her generous drawing-room windows in Seaton Carew, now held little interest. With the outside world lost to her, the thoughts that she'd wanted to keep at bay crowded her mind like gatecrashers at a party.

It was all John's fault. He'd dreamed up the plan in the first place and he'd then blown it all to pieces by handing himself in. All through their relationship he'd charged into things, only consulting her as an afterthought, trying to persuade her retrospectively that he'd been right. And now look where they'd ended up!

In her organised, doctor's receptionist mind she conveniently filed away the small detail that, while John may have instigated the plan, it was she who kept it going. All the lies she'd told, even while he wasn't there — lie upon lie, layered one on top of the other, similarly to when she used to make papier mâché with the kids from strips of newspaper — were carefully buried and forgotten. She'd been a victim, she reminded herself. Now all she had to do was convince the court of that.

The more she concentrated on her own status as victim the better she was able to push aside other, darker thoughts that crowded her head whenever she relaxed her guard. Those thoughts were of Mark and Anthony, the sons that she'd lied to consistently for five and a half long years; the sons she'd allowed to mourn a father who, far from being dead, was actually just feet away; the sons whose tears she'd witnessed in silence, and whose enduring grief she'd observed, knowing all the time that she could bring their sorrow to an end with just a few words.

She'd had no reply to the letter she sent Mark. He'd been so supportive of her after John's disappearance. She knew he must feel betrayed beyond measure. Anthony, less introspective and intense than his brother, had written back to say that he couldn't face talking to her right now, that it was all too soon, all too raw.

In a way her insistence on a trial was her offering to them, the two sons she'd wronged. If only she could convince the jury that she'd been forced to tell all those lies, that she'd been manipulated by a domineering husband she couldn't refuse, surely then her boys would forgive her? Or if not forgive, at least understand.

For more than three decades her life had been constructed around the dual pillars of her two great roles as wife and mother. Now, with her husband locked away from her, literally and metaphorically, and with her sons refusing to have anything to do with her, nothing was holding up the existence she'd so carefully built up. Instead, alone for the first time ever, she was trying, with shaking arms, to prop up a life that had already started to crumble around her ears.

If she didn't manage to show a jury, and through them her sons, that she'd been coerced into acting in a way that went against every principle she held, she'd be nothing. Not wife, not mother – a shadow woman without substance.

And so she persevered, watching the sky change through her cell window, structuring her life around the visits from her solicitor and trying to keep her fear at bay; waiting, just waiting, for the next chapter to begin.

If ever a movie is made about the Darwins, mature actresses will doubtless fight one another to secure the role of Anne. It's easy to imagine the part being played by someone like Dame Judi Dench, all tightly wrapped misery and eloquent silences. But there cannot be a greater test of acting skill than the one displayed by Anne herself when she walked into Teesside Crown Court in Middlesbrough, Cleveland, at the start of her trial on 14 July 2008, calm and impassive, betraying no hint of the turmoil that must have been going on inside her. No one would have guessed that this neat woman, with her white shirt and pale-blue fleecy top, was fighting to salvage everything she held most dear.

From her position in the dock she tried to look straight ahead, resisting the temptation to glance around the room in search of familiar faces among the gawping, expectant onlookers. Had her sons come, or any of her family?

Dwarfed by the magnitude of the occasion, she cut a small, lonely figure as she listened to the case being put against her. Crown Prosecutor Andrew Robertson QC spelled out the details of the Darwins' financial crisis and of the scheme they concocted to get themselves out of it, pouring scorn on Anne's defence of marital coercion.

'The initial idea may well have been John Darwin's rather than Anne's,' he conceded. 'But, in the Crown's submission, it was a scheme in which Anne Darwin not only played an equal and vital role but it was a role which she played with superb aplomb.'

Mr Robertson painted a picture of a marriage that, far from being unequal, was a loving partnership. John Darwin might have come up with the fake death scheme, but it was Anne who rang the police to report him missing, it was she who told her sons that their father was gone, and she who kept the lie going for five long years.

As Anne listened intently he described how the strait-laced, church-going receptionist who'd never been in trouble before had been instrumental in collecting the insurance money after John's 'disappearance' and in making sure that the money was then dispersed into various bank accounts and finally on to Panama, making it almost impossible to trace.

The Case That Didn't Hold Water

The Anne Darwin he described was sly, manipulative, greedy and utterly without conscience. It was a woman few of her friends or relatives would recognise. As she listened on, giving nothing away, it's unlikely – given her already proven capacity for evolving her story to fit around whatever fresh facts came to light – that she even recognised herself.

It wasn't until Day Two of the trial, as the hitherto oppressive weather over Teesside Crown Court finally broke to allow through some chinks of sunlight, that Anne's composure crumpled. For there, just feet away from her in the witness box, giving evidence against her for the Prosecution, were her beloved sons.

Put yourself, once again, in Anne's sensible flat shoes. The last time she saw her sons had been when they'd hugged and waved her off to her new life in Panama, sad to see her go but oh so proud to have a mother who saw life as an adventure, in spite of all the hardships that had been thrown her way. That had been more than eight months before. The sons who walked into Teesside Crown Court that Tuesday were no longer proud of their mother, a woman who'd cheated the system and lied to them for five and a half years.

When they looked at her, which they often did, it wasn't through eyes soft with love and filial devotion, but eyes that were cold, hard and accusing. She couldn't bear to see the depth of her betrayal reflected back at her through the gaze of the sons she loved. And so she stared straight ahead.

But when Mark took the stand her steely resolve finally failed her. Hearing her elder son describe how the news of his father's disappearance had 'crushed his world', her silver head bowed down, as if finally unable to bear the weight of the guilt she was carrying. Then, when Mark went on to explain how he felt when the infamous photo emerged of his smiling parents, posing with a Panamanian estate agent, while thousands of miles away he and his brother still grieved for their lost father, came the first signs of real emotion as she dabbed away at her tears with a tissue handed to her by one of the security guards next to her.

All the stress of the past five years – all the sleepless nights, the close calls, the times her heart was pounding so hard that she thought it would go straight through her chest – and all for nothing. The money was locked away in Panama, John was locked away in Durham and now her two sons, her pride and joy, had locked themselves off from her. Whatever the outcome of the trial, she had lost everything.

From that Tuesday onwards the media, which up until then had been happy to go along with the idea of John as the main protagonist, with Anne as his faithful sidekick, turned on her. Coverage which before then had largely shown the Darwins as small-time, bumbling but harmless fraudsters now focused on the human cost of their deception. And it was Anne who took the full force of the attack.

On the stand the frail little 56-year-old tried to convince onlookers that she'd been powerless to resist her domineering husband. Her voice, always quiet, seemed to tail off into thin air in the open courtroom and she had to be asked to stand in order that it might carry better.

'I'd always done what John wanted me to do,' she claimed. 'He was telling me what to do and I had no choice.'

The Case That Didn't Hold Water

Another time she asserted: 'Whatever John wanted, John got.'

And yet court observers had heard also how Anne and John had swapped joking emails that clearly showed her to be a loving partner rather than a downtrodden wife. 'Missing you already,' she'd written the night he left Panama for the last time. And they'd heard from her friend Irene Blakemore how convincing Anne had been in her portrayal as a grieving widow despite the fact that John wasn't there at the time. They'd heard how much she'd loved being in Panama and how on-the-ball she'd been about their investments there. Most damningly, they heard how, while claiming to be a loving mother, she had stood by and watched her sons grieve for a man who wasn't dead.

As the proceedings lumbered through that first week, under a largely overcast Middlesbrough sky, the headlines were less about the £250,000 the Darwins had swindled from the insurance companies and more concerned with the heartache they'd inflicted on their sons. From being an almost comedic figure – the innocuous, grey-haired receptionist who fled to Panama to start a new life in the tropics on her husband's ill-gotten gains – Anne Darwin was fast becoming a figure of hate. By Friday, 18 July it was clear that, in the media at least, she would be tried not for being a fraudster, but for being a bad mother.

How long must that following weekend have seemed to Anne, banished to her cell after her moment in the spotlight? With what anguish must she have relived the evidence of her sons? 'Upset, betrayed,' was how Anthony described his feelings on realising he'd been duped by the very people supposed to love him best. How those words must have echoed in Anne Darwin's head as she tossed and turned in the cramped single bed, in itself a painful reminder of the brand-new double back in her Panama apartment, and those mornings when she'd wake up with the equatorial sun slanting in behind the curtain and the ubiquitous sound of the birds outside the bedroom. In prison there were only institutional noises — echoing shouts, scraping trays, heavy footsteps, plus the occasional muffled sound of someone crying behind closed doors.

By the time Monday came around, Anne must have had some sense of foreboding. The weekend's newspapers, bound to keep their counsel until the end of the trial by the laws of sub judice, still managed in their choice of headlines to convey their disapproval. CANOEIST'S WIFE ANNE DARWIN ACCUSED OF "CRUCIFYING HER SONS",' read one. 'ANNE DARWIN TOLD "YOU'VE LIED AND LIED",' intoned another.

But if she felt her world was about to about to come crashing down around her comfortably shod feet, she was not about to let it show. As the closing speeches from both counsels were read out on that interminable Monday she remained impassive. Her defence lawyer tried to paint a picture of a woman so bullied by her domineering husband over the course of their 30-year marriage that she was no longer able to stand up to him. She might have told lies, but it was on John Darwin's instructions.

The Prosecutor, on the other hand, described a woman who'd willingly lied at every turn, changing her story to fit every fresh fact that emerged, a woman so attached to material goods that she'd helped her husband defraud the system so as to hang on to what they had, even though it meant depriving her sons of a father.

For her own part she gave nothing away, keeping her eyes fixed firmly ahead as she listened to the evidence against her, both as a civilian and, more to the point it seemed, as a mother. She'd lied to save her own skin, the Prosecutor alleged, no matter how much it shattered the lives of those closest to her.

The judge's summing-up, the following day, was listened to in exactly the same manner – all four hours of it. This was a 'highly unusual case', Justice Wilkie told the jury, sipping from a glass of milk. It had been 'dramatic and highly charged', but their duty was to put aside 'emotional responses' and consider the evidence.

As Anne Darwin was claiming her husband made her carry out the individual offences, the jury had to be convinced, he told them, that John Darwin had been present on each and every occasion and that she had been 'overborne' by him.

At just after 3pm that Tuesday, the jury retired to consider their verdict. When they were unable to reach a decision after 90 minutes of deliberation, they were sent home until the following day.

That night, she returned to her prison cell knowing there was a very good possibility that this was the last time she'd lie awake, unsure of what was to become of her. By the next night, she might be starting out on a prison sentence or maybe, just maybe (and this was a possibility she hardly dared let herself think), she might be free.

Anne Darwin was a woman who maintained her religious faith even through the backlash of the 1960s and 1970s and the disappointment of having a husband not as overtly devout. Did she, on this last night, pray that whatever force had kept her and John's secret safe for those five long years, would give her protection once more? Did she allow herself to imagine how it would be to walk away from Teesside Crown Court a free woman, partially vindicated to her sons and able to pick up whatever pieces remained of the life she'd once had?

Whatever the case, it's unlikely she slept well that Tuesday night. But the next morning, as usual, she was up early and ready, when the call finally came, to be driven the relatively short distance to Middlesbrough – looking neat, and self-contained, her eyes unreadable behind her large glasses.

As the media representatives and the court officials and public filed into the courtroom there was a noticeable air of purpose and expectation that hadn't been present the previous days. People moved with new resolution, whispering urgently to one another. Inside the building there was a fresh momentum about the proceedings.

Watching the members of the jury arrive and take their seats, Anne smiled shyly at them, perhaps in hope, perhaps in acknowledgement of the difficulty of their task, perhaps just because, as someone used to dealing with the public every working day, it was what she'd been trained to do. But no one met her eye.

And then it was time for the verdicts. As the charges were read out – six of fraud and nine of money laundering – the jury foreman was asked how they found the defendant. And on each charge, the verdict was the same: 'Guilty'.

Fifteen times the word 'Guilty' rang out and each time she betrayed no emotion, gazing woodenly ahead as if waiting at a bus stop rather than listening to the words that would shape the rest of her life. There followed a gap of just over an hour, while Anne, her thought processes numb with shock, struggled to take in what had just happened. How could those 12 people not have seen the ridiculousness of finding her guilty? When would they realise they'd made a mistake? People like her just didn't go to jail.

And then, all of a sudden, it was time to go back into the courtroom for sentencing, and there was John, looking bent and somehow broken – like the paddle from his kayak that had washed ashore the day after his disappearance. The couple who once jokingly called each other 'Sexy Beast' and 'Filthy Rich Gringo' now couldn't bear to look at each other, but stood rigidly in the dock a few feet apart, separated by a burly court official.

I can get through this, Anne repeated to herself over and over. This too shall pass. She clasped her hands in front of her and stared straight ahead as Judge Wilkie described John as the driving force behind the crime, while she was the one who enabled him to keep the scam going.

'In my judgement, you operated as a team, each contributing to the joint venture.'

Now there was only one thing left for the judge to do – pass sentence. In a move that would outrage many legal campaigners, John and Anne Darwin – whose protracted and emotionally costly scam had, in the end, netted them just £250,000 – each received a prison sentence longer than those meted out to many rapists and violent criminals. Because he'd already admitted his guilt and saved the taxpayer from funding an expensive trial, John received six years and three months. Having forced the trial, forced their sons to give evidence and cost the British government a lot of money, Anne was given longer: six years and six months.

Anne sniffed as the sentences were handed down, but somehow

she didn't crumple. As she walked briskly from the dock she didn't even glance up to the public gallery, where, close to the back, her sons Mark and Anthony sat stonily, staring down at the proceedings, while betraying the same lack of emotion as their parents.

Breathing a collective sigh of relief, the police officers who'd worked on the case permitted themselves the briefest of congratulatory pats on the back before announcing the next part of their investigation – to try to reclaim the fraudulently obtained money from the Darwins' accounts in Panama.

It was all over. And yet in another sense, of course, as the shaken middle-aged couple from Hartlepool were driven separately back to their respective prisons, it was only just beginning.

EPILOGUE
THE MAN WHO WASN'T
THERE

A s the wet summer of 2008 gave way to an equally wet autumn there were few visible signs of change in the six and a half years since John Darwin had made his way across the sand with his kayak under his arm.

From the outside, No. 3 The Cliff looked the same as it ever did, with its imposing front door and wrought-iron first-floor balcony.

True, the new owner seemed to have spent a sizeable chunk of his time over the preceeding summer showing TV crews around the inside of the house, the main focus of the tour being the secret doorway between No. 3 and No. 4. And true, many local guesthouses had enjoyed higher-than-average bookings, thanks to curious onlookers and dogged journalists who all wanted to see first-hand where the Darwin Affair unfolded.

But on the whole people here were trying to put the story

behind them. There was, after all, still normal life to be lived here
– jobs to be done, kids to be fed, bills to be paid.

The library on Station Lane, where John, in his crazy full-beard
disguise, used to escape from the straitjacket of No. 3 The Cliff,
was promoting its reading group on the first Monday of every
month. Holy Trinity Primary School had a fresh intake of pupils,
and members of Seaton Carew Golf Club had long since moved on
to other, more pressing topics of conversation.

John and Anne Darwin had both launched appeals – he against
the severity of the sentence, she against both sentence and
conviction. But sometimes it can feel as if the wheels of justice are
moving grindingly slowly. As they readjusted to their new realities
behind bars it must have been galling for the Darwins to know
that, just a short distance away, in what was once intended to be
their dream home, life carried on pretty much as it ever did.

The villas in The Cliff continued to stare implacably out across
the road to the beach beyond. The tide still came in and went out
with reassuring monotony, and the North Sea, into which John
Darwin had pitched his little red kayak more than half a dozen
years before, remained as unpredictable and inscrutable as ever.

People's memories are ruthlessly short. By the time the grey
miserable summer of 2008 dribbled interchangeably into a grey
miserable autumn in Seaton Carew, Anne and John Darwin's
cheesily smiling faces no longer graced the front pages of the
newspapers stuffed in the bin outside the seafront chip shop. With
the news now dominated by the deepening credit crunch and
tumbling house prices, those braving the driving rain on the
promenade had more pressing things on their minds than the

Epilogue

'canoeist' and his wife who'd apparently tried – and failed – to outsmart the system.

Forgotten by the public, disowned by their own sons, the couple who'd dreamed of disappearing off the radar into blessed obscurity had achieved more or less what they set out to do.

Sometimes, as the cliché goes, you really should be careful what you wish for.